Toward Dusk
and
Other Stories

Yoshiyuki Junnosuke

Toward Dusk
and
Other Stories

Yoshiyuki Junnosuke

Translated by
Andrew Clare

and with an introduction by
James Dorsey

Kurodahan Press
2011

Toward Dusk and Other Stories
Yoshiyuki Junnosuke

Translated by Andrew Clare

All stories are copyright Yoshiyuki Junnosuke, and translated
with the permission and encouragement of Honme Mariko.

Translation copyright © 2011 Andrew Clare. First Japanese
publication information is on page 215.
Introduction copyright © 2011 Kurodahan Press.

FG-JP0026-L32
ISBN: 978-4-902075-17-5

KURODAHAN PRESS
Kurodahan Press is a division of Intercom, Ltd.
#403 Tenjin 3-9-10, Chuo-ku, Fukuoka 810-0001 JAPAN
www.kurodahan.com

Acknowledgements

Thanks are due to Edward Lipsett and his team at Kurodahan Press, without whose assistance this book would not have seen the light of day.

I would also like to express my gratitude to John Bester, to whom this book is dedicated, whose superlative rendering of Yoshiyuki's *The Dark Room* into English provided the inspiration for the translations included in the present volume.

Andrew Clare
Manchester, England
October 2011

TABLE OF CONTENTS

Introduction

James Dorsey

As a graduate student in Japanese literature in the United States some years ago a classmate introduced me to the world of Yoshiyuki Junnosuke through the short story "My Bed is a Boat" (Nedai no fune). I was so taken with it that I decided to translate it into English. I passed a copy of that translation to my advisor and asked him to give me his opinion. A week or so later, when I checked back with him, he said, "I didn't have time to compare it carefully against the original, but I will say that I think you capture the essence of Yoshiyuki's work. I say that because your translation, just like the originals I've read in the past, left me desperately wanting to take a shower and scrub myself clean."

He was reacting, of course, to the fact that this story, like so many by this writer, is filled with sticky liquids of all sorts, many of them bodily fluids. They seep in, ooze out, flow through, coagulate on, bead up and drip down in all corners of Yoshiyuki's stories. For example, in the narrative in question, "My Bed is a Boat," the protagonist's daily commute to his teaching job at a girls' school takes him through a dank tunnel made constantly damp by water seeping through its walls. His tedious days at this job are punctuated by visits to the room of the transvestite Misako, and he wakes in her bed one morning to discover that a manly oil has oozed through her makeup to cover her face as she slept. Beside her bed is a vanity packed with "row upon row of glass bottles of all shapes and sizes filled with countless liquids: red, green, milk white, and some clear" (3). While the protagonist of this story waits in vain for his cells to once again "be filled with the juices of youth" (2), Misako takes matters into her own hands by injecting him with a virility-inducing serum from a hypodermic needle. That action complete, she promptly refills and inserts the blood-streaked needle into her own arm. Fluids are so ubiquitous and, for the most part, presented in forms so unappealing throughout the narrative that author Kaikō Ken described the story as one written in "grease" (*abura*, a word used also to refer to oil, lard, fat, and a few other distasteful fluids as well).[1]

For respite from the unpleasant feeling generated by the viscous fluids flowing from all corners of this world, the reader might turn to elements usually associated with cleanliness and purity. These areas, however, have been similarly tainted by the greasy fluids circulating all around them. The sweet young girls in the classroom stare at the protagonist through eyes that are a murky white and somehow lacking any gleam of intelligence. The sea, a vast expanse of water which one might expect to wash all things clean, is here a foul, blackish-blue. The story takes its title and quotes liberally from the nursery rhyme "My Bed is a Boat" included in Robert Louis Stevenson's *Child's Garden of Verses*. In any other context the lines from this nursery rhyme would evoke the pleasant image of an imaginative child bringing toys under the blankets in order to turn bedtime into an adventure, but in Yoshiyuki's story these same lines cannot but be read differently: the imagination is being deployed to buttress the fading glories of an aging transvestite and the "adventures" are all of a sexual nature, complete with "toys" of a different sort incorporated in desperate attempts to intensify the titillation. Nothing in the story is impervious to the flow of Yoshiyuki's sticky, murky fluids. An English translation of "My Bed is a Boat" is included in the

---

1 Quoted in Takahashi Hiromitsu, *Yoshiyuki Junnosuke: Hito to bungaku* (Tokyo: Bensei shuppan, 2007), 90.

companion volume to this book,[2] but the stories in the current volume also offer landscapes and bodies similarly dampened by fluids of all sorts. Yoshiyuki's fiction does indeed sometimes make one want to take a shower and scrub thoroughly.

The sticky moisture of a Yoshiyuki story is often accompanied by unvarnished images of natural phenomena. Nature in Yoshiyuki's mind is not linked to red and orange sunsets or pristine mountain streams; to him it is gritty elements such as withered leaves hanging limp like "overly boiled spinach" ("Flowers," 97) or a flower stigma damp with "mucilage" ("Straw Wedding Ceremony," 64). Such organic matter combines with the aforementioned moisture to imply fecundity, fertility, an atmosphere conducive to growth and new life. On the grand scale Yoshiyuki's literature does suggest these things. Disappointments, ruptures, and disasters of both personal and national proportions come and go, and yet somehow life goes on. These continuities, however, unfold in the background. In the foreground are the delicate shifts in human psychology that occur as human relationships run their courses. At this level the aura of moist fecundity is always ruptured, undermined, or compromised as would-be lovers are pushed apart or adolescents on the brink of sexual awakening are left frustrated and confused.

"My Bed is a Boat" is a perfect case in point. The narrator, a teacher, moonlights as a translator, rendering into Japanese an article about farming implements used to till the soil. Fertility is the issue he grapples with intellectually in that work, and in indirect ways the idea looms over his relationship with the transvestite Misako. Obviously procreation is not a possibility for the two, but this fact serves only to increase the importance of them having a satisfying physical encounter of some sort, no matter how fleeting. However, though fluids and moisture abound in the pages of "My Bed is a Boat," the union that these would seem to portend is time and again

2 Yoshiyuki Junnosuke, *Fair Dalliance: Fifteen Stories by Yoshiyuki Junnosuke*, translated by Lawrence Rogers (Fukuoka, Japan: Kurodahan Press, 2011).

interrupted by the emergence of an obstacle that upsets both characters equally: Misako's penis. Though by all outward appearances a female, Misako continues to experience an erection when sexually stimulated, and its arrival so surprises and disturbs the protagonist that each time he abruptly breaks off their embrace.

In the closing passages of the story the schoolteacher muses on a way to overcome this obstacle: he imagines that pouring a bottle of expensive imported perfume over Misako's engorged penis might somehow erase that last obstacle to a pleasurable corporeal union of some sort. Within this daydream all the conventional elements of a fecund sexual relationship are present. There is the aura of organic life and fertility in the form of the farm implement translation; there is a magnificent penis; there is a person overflowing with feminine charms; there is an elegant bottle of perfume. While these elements titillate the reader with the promise of a fine sexual dalliance and perhaps even hint at procreation, events do not unfold this way. The configuration of the individual elements will simply not allow it: the penis is wielded by the transvestite, and the perfume is splashed about by the male teacher. Even the promise of fecundity introduced by the translation is recognized, in retrospect, as having been a red herring: at the completion of the job, the teacher's shaky command of English left him unsure whether the plowing described was even possible.

In these respects "My Bed is a Boat" is typical of much of Yoshiyuki's fiction. Indeed, in his oeuvre there are precious few instances of sexual encounters that satisfy or fulfill the characters in a conventional sense. Always there is a deferral, a transference, or an inversion, and oftentimes it seems that this abnegation is itself what provides the deepest pleasure. Or, perhaps, it may be that the sidestepping of conventional sexual intercourse is the precondition that makes it possible for Yoshiyuki's protagonists (many of whom seem to be alter egos of the author) to enter into relationships in the first place.

POET, SCHOLAR AND CRITIC Ueda Miyoji identifies this dynamic in Yoshiyuki's work, though he casts it in terms of human relationships rather than sexual intimacy:

> A distinguishing characteristic of Yoshiyuki is his fear and resistance to relationships. Yoshiyuki finds unbearable even the relationships between men and women that are difficult to avoid because they are so deeply rooted in sexual instincts. He finds them unbearable because they lead to the marriages and families that envelop us in the web of social connections and because they are linked to the preservation and development of the human race.[3]

Yoshiyuki's aversion to those relationships, Ueda continues, prompts him to limit his emotions to "fondness" (*ki ni iru*) rather than allowing himself to fall in love (*ai suru*).[4]

While the level of emotional involvement is difficult to measure in the characters, the nature of their sexual engagement points to a similar psychology. For all the sexually charged encounters included in the stories collected in this volume, there are but two accounts of conventional sexual intercourse. One is found in an oft-referenced section of this volume's title work "Toward Dusk." Sasa, the married, middle-aged protagonist spends many an evening away from his wife and daughter, opting instead to be in the company of the twenty-three-year-old Sugiko. Sasa often escorts her to love hotels during their rendezvous, but the only genuine intercourse that takes place occurs in a vision of sorts that comes to Sasa while in Sugiko's arms. He imagines

> a rocky desert of red soil stretching out around him. With his back to the entrance of their cliff cave home, with his body on top of a woman or perhaps behind one in the posture of an animal, he performed the sexual act, wide-eyed, all the while

3 Ueda Miyoji, "Sei o jiku to suru reisei na jinsei kansatsusha," in *Yoshiyuki Junnosuke zenshū*, vol. 1 (Tokyo: Kōdansha, 1983), 362.

4 Ibid. The importance of this distinction in Yoshiyuki's work is also highlighted by Tsuge Teruhiko in "Yoshiyuki Junnosuke to kindai bungaku: tokaisei o megutte," in *Yoshiyuki Junnosuke: Sono sei no fūkei*, special issue of *Kokubungaku kaishaku to kanshō*, vol. 40, no. 11 (Oct. 1975), 128.

> watching for signs of attack by beasts or reptiles. Eyes tightly
> shut, the woman leaves everything to the man. The nearby
> grass sways in the wind. The man tenses for an instant, the
> woman paying no heed (189).

This scene represents sexual intercourse as a primal act in a primitive setting. The larger context for this vision, however, makes it clear that it does not represent the transcendence of societal taboos or personal inhibitions in an act that joins two individuals together in a most basic, corporeal manner. Instead, in Sasa's mind at least, this sexual act is associated directly with procreation, particularly procreation as he believes it is perceived by a woman. Sasa imagines such intercourse stimulating a flow of "primeval blood" (189) in the woman; he also assumes it triggers in the woman a belief that her relationship with that particular partner is somehow special (189).

In short, conventional heterosexual intercourse in Sasa's mind is inextricably tied to procreation and a permanent relationship between the partners. The trajectory is clearly toward marriage, domestic life, and family: just moments after Sasa's vision of intercourse in front of the cave, he suddenly remembers that he has left his dog in the care of a veterinarian and it would soon be coming home. What could better illustrate domesticity than the image of a man at home with his dog curled at his feet? Such domesticity, with himself the designated provider and protector, is what Sasa associates with sexual intercourse, and it inevitably provokes in him the same physical reaction: the withering of his erection (189). This reaction suggests that for all his professed desires for actual intercourse with Sugiko, Sasa is ultimately happier with the *simulation* of it that he performs with her. Clinging tenaciously to her virginity as narrowly conceived, Sugiko has refused to engage in intercourse with Sasa. She does, however, enthusiastically pursue every other option open to them, and their trysts in love hotels typically end with Sasa inserting his penis between Sugiko's clamped thighs, an area that has been moistened with olive oil from a bottle that Sasa carries in his breast pocket. In the end, it is the deferral of the act of intercourse that allows Sasa to indulge his sexual desires; it is only the simulation of the act that allows him sexual pleasures untainted by the specter of home, family, and the domestic life.

This physical and psychological aversion to domesticity haunts the sexual dalliances of Sasa and many of Yoshiyuki's characters. Its source is hinted at in the second depiction of conventional heterosexual intercourse included in this volume of short stories. It appears in "Straw Wedding Ceremony," and it is prefaced with a striking portrayal of precisely the kind of moist, organic fecundity that was identified above as a distinguishing characteristic of Yoshiyuki's fiction. The scene comes in the form of a flashback, a return to a day during wartime when the protagonist's house is destroyed in an air raid and he flees the conflagration with the mysterious woman named Mio. They lie down together in a meadow to rest and the protagonist tears open Mio's blouse to reveal "a pair of peach-blossom pink nipples" that point into the blue sky (64). Their attention is soon turned to a single red wildflower blooming beside them, a miraculous flash of color in a monochrome landscape of burnt ruins and ash-colored debris. Lying on the ground, the protagonist views the flower from but inches away. He notices that the

> tips of the radially aligned stamens were dusted with a crust of dark brown pollen. In the middle of the radial, the stigma of the pistil shone smoothly as if it were glass melted in a fire. Enticed by its colour, my finger was drawn towards the stigma. When the tip of my finger touched it very gently, it was moistened with mucilage and trailed a long thread. . . . I gazed at my wet fingertip and then unhurriedly drew near the dark brown pollen on the stigma. As I did so, Mio . . . put my wet finger in her mouth and applied her teeth to it vigorously. Locked in that position, we collapsed amongst the grasses and, like animals of a human size, we entered a state of sexual intercourse all too easily" (64).

TOWARD DUSK

The image of Mio's blossom-like nipples fades quickly into a close-up of an actual flower, the details of which are rendered in a sexual manner reminiscent of a Georgia O'Keeffe painting. Doing her one better, though, Yoshiyuki has his protagonist's phallic-like finger probe the flower and caress it, drawing moisture in the form of "mucilage." Having been focused very tightly on the finger and flower, the point of view then recedes, first to include Mio as she takes the phallus/finger into her mouth, and then still further to include the humans in first an embrace and then in the act of intercourse itself.

This scene shares much with the vision narrated in "Toward Dusk." Both take place in a primal landscape and both describe the sexual act as animal-like. The differences between the two, however, are perhaps more significant than these similarities. Unlike the depiction in "Toward Dusk," the intercourse in "Straw Wedding Ceremony" is not linked by association or narrative sequencing to menstruation, procreation, domesticity or family. In a sense it is a "pure" sexual act—it occurs spontaneously and with both participants living entirely in the moment. It is neither colored by social and national agendas nor charged with an ideological significance. As such, this scene occupies a rather unique place within Yoshiyuki's body of work. It may well be that it is the timing of the story that makes this depiction possible. The story "Straw Wedding Ceremony" is the oldest in this collection and one of Yoshiyuki's earliest, dating to 1948. The scene in question, too, is set at a significant moment in time: it occurs in 1945, during the saturation bombings of Tokyo in the chaotic final months of the war.[5] Therefore, both this seminal episode and the moment at which it was recorded occur during a window of time when the wartime rhetoric no longer held sway and the postwar belief system had not yet gelled. The chaos and un-

5 This piece of the story seems based at least partially on Yoshiyuki's personal experience. The home that he shared with his mother and a one-time assistant at her beauty parlor was destroyed during the 25 May 1945 air raids. See Takahashi Hiromitsu, *Yoshiyuki Junnosuke: Hito to bungaku* (Tokyo: Bensei shuppan, 2007), 32-34.

certainty that ruled from the closing years of the war through the years immediately following the surrender generated an ideological moratorium of sorts. It was the one time when, for Yoshiyuki, sex could simply be sex.

At all other times of his life Yoshiyuki existed within constellations of powerful social pressures. Born in April 1924, he came of age during the years of Japan's expanding militarism and imperialism. The talk in those years focused on the need for wholesome living, Spartan lifestyles, selfless sacrifice, and spiritual purity. Like all of his generation Yoshiyuki was exposed to this wartime propaganda and, regardless of his personal proclivities, ultimately resigned to living in accordance with it, at least on the surface. Military service was expected of all men, of course, and Yoshiyuki was actually drafted twice. The first time was in August 1944. Yoshiyuki returned to his ancestral home in Okayama and entered the barracks after a tearful parting from family and relatives there. Before the week was out, however, he was home again, discharged after a physician determined him medically unfit due to respiratory problems. Though he would later be plagued by just such health problems, this early diagnosis seems to have been mistaken.[6] In the spring of 1945 he was again drafted and determined fit for duty, but the massive air raids on Tokyo and the end of the war came before he was inducted.

The indoctrination to the state's agenda left its mark on all members of that generation, and the psychological repercussions were surely even more complicated in cases such as Yoshiyuki's. He had, after all, been first primed for military service and then denied the opportunity to fulfill that destiny. Such lack of closure and the enduring anxieties that it fuels may partially account for Yoshiyuki's lifelong devotion to the demimonde, hedonism, and sexual adventure—all pursuits frowned upon by the wartime state. Making them the center

6 Biographical information on Yoshiyuki is based largely on that found in Takahashi Hiromitsu, *Yoshiyuki Junnosuke: Hito to bungaku* (Tokyo: Bensei shuppan, 2007). Information on this period of Yoshiyuki's life can be found on pages 30-31 and 221.

of his literary universe was one way of signaling his resentment of that oppressive agenda foisted on him by that tyrannical regime.

Yoshiyuki's sensitivity to ideological manipulation, however, seems to have made him equally leery of ideals promoted in postwar Japan. Ironically, one can discern within the postwar discourse some echoes of wartime rhetoric. While the wartime call for women to "produce and give birth" (*umeyō, fuyaseyō*) was not, of course, repeated after 1945, in its attempts to quell the social unrest growing in the run up to the 1960 renewal of the U.S.–Japan Joint Security Treaty (*Ampo*), the government did increasingly push its citizens to sacrifice for the nation by uniting behind its pursuit of economic growth.[7] As Elise Tipton notes in her history of modern Japan, during the decades of high-speed economic growth that began in the late 1950s,

> concentration on 'GNP first' was represented as a new national goal towards which all Japanese could and should aim. The state called upon Japanese to work hard and sacrifice in the interest of GNP growth much as it prodded them to work selflessly during the war. [Prime Minister Hayato] Ikeda's Income Doubling Plan was intended to deflect the public's attention from the divisive and disruptive political conflicts of the previous decade and to bring peace to the workplace so that production could grow.[8]

The sacrifice called for included a carrot at the end of the stick for the nation's citizens: the promise of the "bright life" (*akarui seikatsu*), a comfortable lifestyle characterized largely by consumer goods for the home. Inspired by images of American affluence as seen in TV series such as *I Love Lucy* and *Father Knows Best*, Japanese nationals aspiring to the middle class concentrated on obtaining the "three imperial treasures" of the postwar consumer's "bright life": a washing machine, a re-

7 See, for example, Mariko Tamanoi, *Under the Shadow of Nationalism* (Honolulu: University of Hawai'i Press, 1998), 164-165.

8 Elise Tipton, *Modern Japan: A Social and Political History* (London: Routledge, 2002), 178.

frigerator, and a television.[9] Even as this list evolved during the course of Japan's economic miracle, the focus was always on items intended for *domestic or family use*. The updated version of the list popular in the 1960s maintained this focus; it was an age when the newly emergent middle class was coaxed into desiring the "three Cs": a car, a cooler (i.e. air conditioner), and a color television.[10] In short, attention was focused on the new middle class, and the life courses of all would-be members were largely dictated by the requirements of gaining entrance to it.

The key to this "bright life" was smooth passage into a prestigious university and then up through the ranks of a promising company. The competition was such that success required contributions from all members of a family. Stay-at-home mothers were better able to coach their sons through school; they could also simultaneously train their daughters in the skills needed to one day marry and maintain a household that would support a similarly upwardly mobile businessman. The whole system was, of course, designed to support the bread-winning husband, whose salary also funded the endeavor. His career success demanded long hours in the office and weekends on the golf course consolidating relationships with superiors and clients. In short, buying into the postwar dream of suburban middle class "bliss" meant men were agreeing to a lifetime yoked to the companies that employed them.

The attitudes toward conventional intercourse exhibited by Yoshiyuki's characters seem very much a response to this postwar configuration of social pressures. While sex could be simply sex during the closing days of the war and in the confusion of the early occupation years, once the call of the middle class began to resound in all corners, to engage in sexual intercourse, with its potential to lead to procreation and family,

9 See Tipton, 171. Though Tipton suggests that one of these prized consumer goods was a vacuum cleaner, most histories of the Shōwa era list the three I have mentioned here.

10 Tipton, 182.

was to make oneself complicit in the myth of the happy middle class. Considering the length and intensity of the commitment that this might entail, it is perhaps not surprising that protagonists like Sasa prefer the option of simulated sex—even if it meant using olive oil on thighs clamped shut.

Yoshiyuki Junnosuke was not, of course, the only writer to attempt the construction of a realm that rejected the discourse of wartime Japan without surrendering to the bland, middle-class consumer capitalism of the postwar period.[11] As different as his fiction and lifestyle were, contemporary Mishima Yukio (1925-1970) sought his own path between the Scylla and Charybdis of these poles. While Yoshiyuki portrayed a variety of sexual pleasures and sexually charged relationships that resisted incorporation into either ideological system, Mishima's solution was a resurrection and rehabilitation of wartime imagery and sensibilities as part of an effort to invigorate what he saw as the flagging of postwar aesthetics.[12] Another writer who grappled with these poles was Sakaguchi Ango (1906-1955). His bombastic early postwar works such as "Discourse on Decadence" (Darakuron, 1946) were driven as much by a repulsion for the wholesomeness of the U.S. occupation forces with their "rationed freedom" (haikyū sareta jiyū) as they were by a resentment of the enforcement of abstemious lifestyles by the wartime regime.[13] Ango chose to champion the idea of

11 For an introduction to Yoshiyuki's relationship to his cohort of writers (Mishima Yukio, Endō Shūsaku, Abe Kōbō, Kojima Nobuo, Shōno Junzō, Shimao Toshio, and Yasuoka Shōtarō, among others), see Okuno Takeo, "Yoshiyuki bungaku no genpūkei," in Yoshiyuki Junnosuke zenshū, vol. 2 (Tokyo: Kōdansha, 1971), 307-308.

12 I am thinking here, especially, of his 1961 short story "Yūkoku." For an English translation, see: "Patriotism," trans. Geoffrey W. Sargent, in Death in Midsummer and Other Stories (Tokyo: Charles E. Tuttle Company, Inc., 1966), 93-118.

13 This reading of Ango can be found eloquently expounded in Alan Wolfe, "From Pearls to Swine: Sakaguchi Ango and the Humanity of Decadence," in Marlene J. Mayo, J. Thomas Rimer, and H. Eleanor Kerkham, eds, War, Occupation, and Creativity: Japan and East Asia 1920-1960 (Honolulu: University of Hawai'i Press, 2001), 360–80. The phrase "rationed freedom" was coined by philosopher Kawakami Tetsutarō (1902-1980). On this aspect of the occupation, see John W. Dower, Embracing Defeat: Japan in the Wake of WW II (New York: W. Norton & Co, 1999), 70.

"decadence" (*daraku*), and some of what he saw in this stance anticipated Yoshiyuki's exploration of sexual pleasures. However, in his writing Ango was ultimately deploying the idea of decadence in a philosophical manner in order to undermine superficial appeals to the higher human qualities, and in this sense he was advancing a sort of moral agenda of his own. Yoshiyuki, for his part, however, dallies in decadence without ever succumbing to the temptation to theorize it. His critique of wartime and postwar ideologies is, therefore, in a certain sense the more radical.

Yoshiyuki's stubborn resistance to both the wartime model of restraint combined with self-sacrifice and the postwar myth of middle class bliss is evident in most of the stories in this collection. While the family units at the core of both worldviews haunt many of the works, the real "action" of the stories inevitably unfolds in places where far more primal urges reign supreme. The picture-perfect house and domestic life of the young wife in "At the Aquarium" is a fine example. She shares a Western-style home in a quiet suburb with her husband, a company employee ten years her senior. He is so devoted to her that he even arranges for them to take lessons in ballroom dance. They are blessed with a child. But while the story reveals and circles around this oasis of the Shōwa dream of middle-class bliss, nothing important actually takes place within it. Though led right up to the doorstep, readers are never taken *inside* the house. And the important conversations that drive the story take place instead in the sort of locale that Yoshiyuki so much prefers to the sterile world of domestic bliss. The housewife and her young student admirer meet, and her story begins to unfold, in a locale that is the polar opposite of that ostensibly bright and cheery home: the dark, dank aquarium which proves to be teeming with life while appearing at first glance to be all but empty. For Yoshiyuki's protagonists, life is that which unfolds in a realm divorced from, or parallel to, the site of familial life.

The same is true of "Toward Dusk." The protagonist Sasa seems to embody the dream of Shōwa success. All indications are that he has a good-paying company job that allows him the luxury of his own home. He is married, with a daughter in middle school. He even owns his own car, one of the "three Cs" that distinguish the new middle class. However, these are not the marks of Yoshiyuki's Shōwa, and no more than a brief scene or two takes place in Sasa's home, that citadel of domesticity. The extent to which he loathes such homes is fully revealed in his attitude toward Sugiko's relationship to her genteel family. Sugiko and her friends are, with but one or two exceptions, generally described as being from respectable families (140), and Sugiko's desire to maintain her virginity seems rooted in her belief that it is a precondition to fulfill her destiny to someday form a "respectable family" of her own. While part of the narrative evokes these ideals, Sasa seems bent on undermining them. In one scene Sasa has just driven Sugiko home in his car after yet another of their amorous rendezvous. The night drive has tired him, and he stops the car to rest for a moment. He reaches around Sugiko's neck and pulls her head towards him, signaling his desire for her to perform fellatio. The depiction is rather graphic, with Sasa expecting that once again "when he came, she would close her eyes and gulp it down, and the smell of semen would linger a while in her mouth and on her lips" (175). Sugiko resists Sasa's advance, and he soon realizes why:

> She was afraid of going into her parents' house with that pungent smell clinging to her lips.
> The lights inside her home were warm and inviting, and the outline of her family, whom Sasa had never met, was filled in with black. Sugiko would go into the house wearing an air of innocence, her lips clamped tightly shut to prevent that odour rising up from her stomach.
> Sasa was wildly excited as he imagined that scene. He applied still more pressure and tried to draw her to him (176).

The passage makes clear that part of the appeal of the act to Sasa is the fact that Sugiko's fellatio represents for him a way of striking back at the quiet domestic bliss that he imagines behind the doors of her "warm and inviting" suburban home. Fellatio is for him a sexual act that threatens the peace and stability of that middle-class myth while, importantly, risking neither conception nor the type of attachment that conventional intercourse engenders in a woman (at least as Sasa imagines it). Intercourse is, in fact, such a threat to Sasa that its occurrence marks the beginning of the end of his relationship with Sugiko. Significantly, he penetrates her only inadvertently, finding himself suddenly inside her when intending only to insert his penis one final time between her olive oil-covered thighs. Nevertheless, this development initiates the changes in Sugiko that will lead to her separation from Sasa and, presumably, her entrance into middle-class domesticity.

The impending transformation into a wife and mother that erases Sugiko from Sasa's life is echoed in the story "Burning Dolls." Here the transformation is played out by the bar hostess Asako. Two men compete for her attention, and she is buffeted about between them much like the mannequins of the story. We see in the tale something of the misogyny that not infrequently colors parts of Yoshiyuki's oeuvre. By the end of this story Asako has disappeared, vanished without a trace. The men who had vied for her affections meet by chance, and they discuss her disappearance. One says, "I heard she got married. I gather it was an arranged marriage to a steady company employee" (10). In Yoshiyuki's world this choice to immerse oneself in the domesticity of the Shōwa dream is, in effect, to erase oneself. Asako's marriage, like marriage for most all the women in Yoshiyuki's fiction, removes her as a possible object of sexual dalliance, thereby erasing her identity entirely. Wanting somehow to retrieve her, resurrect her, one of the men speculates that perhaps she has in fact *not* married and lives instead in some secret room in a corner of the city waiting for a tryst with the other man. Women exist either as objects for potential sexual encounters, or not at all.

The fluids, organic smells, and sexual tensions of the story "Midnight Stroll" open it to an interpretation from this perspective as well. In this piece a university student jousts for psychological advantage with the widowed, middle-aged landlady of his boarding house. Wanting to avoid a confrontation over something so trivial as noisy late-night trips downstairs to the toilet, the student picks his footing carefully, hoping to avoid the spots on the stairs that creak. To his dismay, however, at the foot of the stairs he all but collides with the frumpy landlady as she too shuffles towards the toilet. She insists, twice, that he go first, and as he edges past her in a hallway so narrow that she must turn sideways to allow him passage, his nose is tickled by a "feminine odour, mingled in with the fragrance of perfume" (*kōsui ni majitta onna no nioi*). Though Yoshiyuki does not mention it explicitly, those familiar with old Japanese homes and the septic systems that serviced them will instinctively add to this mix the stench of feces from the toilet itself. Though there is perfume there to entice, in the end it serves mostly to accentuate the putrid vapors of the toilet and the musky smell of middle-aged womanhood. The phrase rendered as "feminine odour" might also be phrased less delicately as "the smell of a woman." It is not surprising that the assault on his olfactory senses combined with the landlady standing guard outside the toilet door render the student ultimately unable to answer nature's call. He retreats back up to his room and, too intimidated by the corporeal presence of his landlady to head downstairs again, he takes the only option left him—he pisses out the window.

This residence is not the middle-class home filled with ever more fancy electronic goods bringing the "bright life" to a nuclear family. Rather, it is a structure housing a widow, her son, and a boarder; it is brimming with organic smells, bodily fluids, and sexual tensions. Though not a snapshot of the Shōwa dream, for Yoshiyuki it holds some authentic promises of its own. Desperate for income, the landlady begins working in a cabaret. On her very first day she brings gentlemen customers home with her, a situation so disconcerting to the student lodger that he embarks on an all-night "midnight stroll," returning only as the sun rises the next day:

> My skin was sticky with sweat and dew from walking around all night. Entering the house I headed straight for the washroom. Though I called it the washroom, it was really the kitchen sink, and it was there that I suddenly came face to face with my landlady. Her eyes were bloodshot with fatigue and alcohol, and her face swollen. . . . All I thought was that perhaps even my landlady . . . would have a more meaningful life opening up before her (85).

Only by resisting the pull of the myth of domestic bliss, only by immersing herself in the messy world of human needs and desires does the landlady have hope of redemption.

The story "The Molester" also escorts the reader directly into a home, and here too it is one with none of the personal warmth and creature comforts associated with the "bright life" of late Shōwa Japan. Part of this story takes place on a humid summer day with a thunderstorm raging outside as three middle-aged men congregate in a tiny, dilapidated room attached to a ramshackle dentist's office on the wrong side of town. They sit on the tatami floor, huddled over a bowl of dry peanuts and some lukewarm beer that sits on a low table. To quiet the room the electric fan has been shut off, and surely the windows have been closed. Though dusk is turning the room dark, the men do not notice as they sit quietly, straining to make out the sounds emanating from the tape recorder, also on the table. The tape is part of Tanaka's "unprecedented international research" on "sensual sounds" (14) emitted by women in the throes of passion. The tapes are silent for up to twenty minutes at a stretch, but the men remain stoically hushed, intent on not missing the few cries of ecstasy that they desperately believe will soon arrive. Readers are told that the men are sweating in the claustrophobic heat of the sealed room, and, just as they struggle to interpret the sounds and imagine the scene, in our own mind's eye we work to flesh out the picture: they are sexually aroused as they listen, and this psychological state augments their production of sweat, making it fall from their brows onto the tabletop and perhaps even the tape recorder itself. The tense scene becomes doubly comic when we discover the real contents of the recordings they listen to so eagerly. It is not the happy home of affluent postwar Japan, but this version of Yoshiyuki's damp, sexually charged domain is also so much more human.

Though known and celebrated for tales like these and his narratives of prostitutes and profligacy, Yoshiyuki is also surprisingly adept at portraying children on the cusp of adolescence and adolescents on the brink of adulthood. In this volume we see such depictions in both "Voice of Spring" and "A Bad Summer." The latter story features Ichirō, a fourth grade schoolboy, and surrounds him with the moist, organic imagery that is one of Yoshiyuki's trademarks. Spending the summer at the seaside with two older uncles, both university students, Ichirō finds himself both flattered and confused by the attention paid him by the young women in their circle of friends. Hoping to gain favor with the uncles, the women fawn over Ichirō, some even offering to carry him around piggyback. Ichirō buries his head in their hair, titillated by the "bittersweet odour" (112) that triggers some long-forgotten memories, perhaps of his mother. By accident Ichirō discovers that he will usually be forgiven if, in his attempts to steady himself on their backs, his hands "accidentally" find their way to the young women's breasts. Yoshiyuki leaves his mark on this sexual awakening a few pages later when little Ichirō finds himself alone on a boat with a swimming instructor. The instructor has seen him with the young women and seizes the opportunity to teach him a lesson. The instructor

> bent over and scooped up a clump of brown seaweed from the surface of the sea close to the boat. Dozens of small, spin-

dle-shaped, dark brown seeds clung to it.

Suddenly pressing the dripping wet weed into Ichirō's face, the instructor laughed again. "Ichirō, you must practice your swimming more," he scolded, scrubbing the mass across Ichirō's face.

He pressed it slowly at first and then with force. The scent of the ocean mingled with the smell of the seaweed assaulted Ichirō's nostrils. Just at that moment, he sensed another odour mixed in with that smell. Or perhaps it had emanated from the strength of the instructor's pressing hand—he wasn't sure which. It was that same dark, mysterious smell (116).

The "dark, mysterious smell" is, of course, that which Ichirō detected in the young women gathering around his uncles. This incident on the boat links his clumsy, surreptitious pawing of these women with the dank, slimy seaweed, casting an entirely unpleasant tone over young Ichirō's sexual awakening. In classic Yoshiyuki style the story is full of moisture and the organic, and the manner in which these things are linked to sexuality often leaves one feeling uncomfortable and somehow grimy.

This sensibility, however, should be placed in the context of the social pressures for middle-class conformity that weighed heavily on many during the postwar decades in which Yoshiyuki produced most of his literature. Within that context it becomes clear that the sticky fluids, the messy instances of organic life, and most of all the sexual titillations that fly in the face of conventional conceptions of "healthy" romances are a mode of resistance to the two dominant ideologies that surrounded Yoshiyuki during his lifetime. Ultimately, the sterile bourgeois values promoted to further the postwar economic recovery proved almost as stifling as the chaste and frugal stoicism demanded by the wartime state. Though his literature may sometimes leave us feeling grimy and in need of a shower, Yoshiyuki opens up a world that resists such social forces, and by reminding us of a range of human behaviors that polite society would prefer to ignore he makes us all perhaps a little more human.

Burning Dolls

人形を焼く

Placing a chair in the middle of the large room, Mita sat down and waited for Imura to return home.

"Mr. Imura will be back very soon now."

The young man in the student's uniform had made the announcement and then disappeared, and an hour had gone by since Mita had been left sitting alone in the room. During that time, the sun had begun to set, and the room had started to grow dark.

The glabrous skin of the naked woman standing nearby emerged pale from the midst of the gloomy space. Four or five arms and legs had been wrenched off and lay piled in one corner on the boarded floor.

With the tip of his finger Mita stroked the woman's shoulder; it was dry and cold to the touch. One arm was extended downwards, with its fingertips bent back a little, while the other arm was bent slightly at the elbow.

Her lips were slightly parted, as if she was about to smile, but her eyes were cold. The bridge of the nose, with its narrow, frigid lines. The cold private parts, devoid of a crack.

The room was quiet; he couldn't hear a sound. Mita felt as though he was starting to recall something, but the thing in his mind failed to take shape. The tedium and the moment when he felt something was about to happen passed.

The ceiling light suddenly came on, and a strong brightness filled the room. The door opened, and a man wearing a home-spun suit came in.

"Oh! You're here."

"I tried going to your house, but they said you'd be here."

"I hope I haven't kept you. The light wasn't even on. . . ."

"Now you mention it, it has gone dark."

"Lost in thought, were you? Surrounded by all these naked women."

While speaking to Mita, Imura seized hold of the arm of the woman next to Mita and raised it firmly. With a creaking noise, the pale, shining arm moved up in the air.

"You've come at just the right time, you realise. I was thinking of getting in touch with you sometime soon. I'm holding a memorial service for the mannequins this Sunday. I'm going to line up the old ones on the beach and burn them. It should be a lot of fun. We'll have some drinks and enjoy ourselves. A lot of the girls from the bar said they'd come along, too."

"You're going to burn these dolls?"

Once again, Mita touched the shoulder of the woman nearby.

"No. I've only just made these. The old ones are crammed into the storeroom next door. I'll take them to K coast in the truck. How about it? Will you come?"

Although Imura was a sculptor, as a sideline he had a small factory that manufactured mannequins. He loaned them to department stores and shops and places like that, and they would soon return covered with scratches. Those dolls that couldn't be repaired were placed in the storeroom. And when it was full to overflowing, it was necessary to incinerate them in a sort of memorial service.

"Sounds like fun," said Mita.

Imura said, "And to crown it all, Asako's coming along as well. I'm head-over-heels in love with her. I'm so in love with her I don't know what to do."

Imura was in the habit of saying that recently.

Asako was a hostess at 'A' Bar. When Mita heard Imura say such things he felt utterly miserable.

AFTER LEAVING IMURA'S HOUSE, Mita rode a cab for about fifteen minutes before stopping in front of an apartment building.

Walking down the long corridor, he came to a halt in front of one of the rooms. The door was locked, so he took a key out of his pocket. There was a dry sound as the key turned in the lock. He opened the door and, as he did so, he could make out the outline of a woman in the dim light, sitting quietly in a chair.

"Asako."

"You came then, as you said, even though I dislike meeting this way," said the woman, remaining seated. Kneeling down in front of the chair, Mita buried his face between the woman's knees and silently began removing her stockings.

Suddenly Imura's face flashed across his mind, and he felt his conscience pricked. Even before Imura had begun saying things like, "I'm head-over-heels in love with her. I'm so in love with her I don't know what to do," Mita had started seeing Asako like this. Had Imura said something like, "I think I'm going to make her mine," then perhaps he would have been able to say, lightheartedly, "I've beaten you to it."

However, Mita failed to mention it at the time. And now he found himself here, with Asako sitting pale and naked in a chair in the dimly lit room.

"I saw the mannequins just now," he said, catching hold of one of Asako's arms and lifting it slowly up. "When I raise an arm up like this, it makes a squeaking noise."

"I've had enough of meeting like this. You think of me as nothing but a tool."

Without replying, he raised Asako's arm farther still and applied his lips to her armpit.

"Don't," murmured Asako, as she wound her arms around him.

It was the day of the mannequin memorial service. A large number of mannequins were standing in a row at the water's edge on K beach—inorganic matter, and yet their skin had a shining hue, giving the strange impression that they were living human beings.

The party was already under way. Most of those who had gathered were sculptors and painters and the like, and so gradually they let their hair down and had a good time. There were also a fair number of girls from the bar they usually patronised. People threw themselves into the arms of the girls and pressed their cheeks together. Some threw their arms around the naked mannequins and nestled close, cheek against cheek. The drinking party gradually became wilder and wilder.

Before long, people began to pour paint thinner over the mannequins as they stood there by the water's edge. A match was brought close. The mannequins burst into flames, and thick black smoke rose into the air as they began to burn, still standing.

Engulfed in flames, the naked mannequins continued to burn without losing shape. But, before very long, bubbles erupted on the skin, and something boiled on the surface. The faces of the mannequins, glowing red amid the dancing flames, remained expressionless, but their skin was covered in small bubbles, and greasy sweat burst forth.

Surrounded by flames at the water's edge, the mannequins looked as though they were suffering a living agony. Their impassive expressions suggested they were enduring extreme pain. Beyond lay the expanse of the pale, dark sea surging toward the dolls, unceasingly undercutting itself and breaking down into white foam.

"What do you think? It's a pretty sensational sight, isn't it?" said Imura to Mita.

"Those dolls—what are they made of?"

"Paper. I make them with soft cardboard—one layer on top of another, and then the whole lot goes in a mould. Then I spray them with lacquer."

"Paper, you say?"

"That's right, paper. Mita, it doesn't matter what they're made of. A fantastic scene, don't you think?"

Asako stood between them. Then suddenly, without warning, she sprang at Imura, a growl issuing from the back of her throat as she did so. She began attacking him like a ferocious animal.

Restraining her shoulders, Imura tried to push her back, but her arms seemed unusually strong.

Against the backdrop of the red flames, the two silhouettes struggled violently, but it wasn't long before Asako appeared suddenly to lose her strength and tumble down onto the sand.

Pressing her face into the beach, her shoulders shook, and she seemed to be crying. Imura stood there without saying anything, looking dumbstruck and even shamefaced. His necktie had been torn off, and his shirt had a gaping rip in it.

"What did you do to her, Imura?"

"I didn't do anything!"

"But . . ."

"I don't get what this is all about. Why did you suddenly . . . Asako."

"But . . ."

"Hey, Mita. Don't go getting any strange ideas."

Imura appeared perplexed. Mita stared at him fixedly, but he couldn't figure anything out. Had Asako attacked him like that, he was sure he would be only too aware of the reason why. At the same time, he was concerned that what he'd been keeping from Imura would come out into the open now.

Still, he reflected, that would be better than being shrouded in suspicion. Mita looked again at his friend Imura, but he was unable to tell anything for sure.

Mita had arranged to see Asako two days later.

He set out for the apartment—a room that he personally rented. He and Asako would meet in that room on an appointed day each week.

He unlocked the door and opened it, but there was no sign of anyone in the dark room. After waiting in vain, he left the room and paid a visit to Imura's house.

When he laid eyes on Mita, Imura right away said, "Yesterday, Asako came to apologise. She said that while she was watching the dolls burn, she was suddenly beside herself with rage. It seems she wasn't even aware herself why she'd done it."

"But, how could she not know, really? Well, what do you think?"

"Me? There's no reason I would know, is there? I think it's true that she didn't know why herself. It's difficult for someone so innocent to put their finger on a reason that lies dormant deep down inside." Then, Imura added, almost in a murmur, "Now it's come to this, I'm more and more at a loss. Asako has a weak spot for me, you see. . . . It upsets me that you think I'm taking advantage of that."

His words sounded to Mita both naïve and hollow.

"Let me hazard a guess as to why Asako got mad at me."

Imura speculated as follows:

To put the story in concrete terms, he said Mita would need to try and recall 'B,' who had won the Miss Japan contest a few years before. Everyone said, when she won, that she was far more beautiful than any of the contenders who had ever appeared in the Miss Japan contest.

It was said she was sure to finish in the top ranks of the Miss Universe contest in America. A movie company had offered its support. She even cut a record—something to appeal to students, in anticipation of her victory.

However, the contest had an unexpected result, and she was defeated early on in a preliminary contest.

From that day forward, all the help that had been extended to her was withdrawn. The smiling faces too were wiped away. She returned to the airport, where she found precious few people there to welcome her. Her enormous debt remained, and, by all accounts, with her brilliant dream shattered, she went to work as a fashion model. Had 'B' witnessed the spectacle of those mannequins going up in flames, she would probably have relived in an instant the events surrounding the tragic end to her wonderful dream.

And then, all manner of attendant pain and unpleasant memories would likely have surfaced all at once.

The mannequins burned standing up, the heat causing the greasy sweat on the skin to bubble. But once they bent over, they would begin to blacken, and then before long they would tumble to the ground. The sight of those mannequins would have been enough to send her into a rage.

"I think this is like that, only on a smaller scale—a glorious dream and its collapse. It's a common occurrence, you know. But the level of excitement from watching those dolls burn doesn't happen very often. It's no wonder that a really sensitive woman would fly into a rage if she saw a sight like that," said Imura, explaining his supposition.

"So, what do you think, Mita?"

"I've no idea," replied Mita, bluntly.

THE FOLLOWING WEEK, ON the day they'd agreed to meet, Asako was in the apartment.

"What the hell happened the other day?"

"It's your fault, isn't it? I've had enough of seeing you like this. Those dolls burning in the flames—they seemed like they were alive. They turned into me."

"And so, you're saying that's why you got mad and started attacking Imura?"

"It's not Imura. It should have been you. But I went dizzy."

Then, she casually murmured, as if to herself, "They've all got it in for me."

"They?" retorted Mita, sharply.

"I'm sure I never said you were the first man I'd been with."

"Weren't you seeing Imura a long time ago?"

"Mr. Imura? A long time ago? There's no reason why I would have done that, is there?"

"Honestly?"

"Honestly. What gave you that idea?"

Mita kept his mouth shut. Then he roughly tore her clothes off.

"I've had enough of this now. Today's the last time I see you like this," said Asako again.

"You're always saying that, aren't you?"

Mita embraced her.

Asako responded to his advances, and repeated once more, "I mean it. Today's the last time."

What she'd said was true. Each week on the appointed day, Mita went to the empty room and waited in vain for her.

Sitting in the chair, he waited quietly. Suppressing his sense of irritation as he sat there, an interval of calm would unexpectedly visit itself upon him at which point each and every part of Asako's body would appear in his mind and begin to speak tenderly to him. At such times, ambivalent feelings of violent lust and pity would force themselves into his mind, and he would rise from the chair in spite of himself.

He waited on three occasions to no avail.

When he tried going to 'A' Bar, they told him that Asako had been away for quite some time, and Mita had no idea where she lived. On the fourth occasion, that day too he sat in the chair and waited in the gloomy room.

He heard footsteps coming up the stairs. The footsteps—heavy, slow and irregular—drew near along the corridor and stopped outside the door to his room. The doorknob turned, and the door opened outwards.

Pale, velvet light flooded the doorway. For an instant, Mita thought he saw something extremely bulky and ill-shaped confronting him in the doorway. It was a young man carrying a naked mannequin. He placed the mannequin on the floor with care. The doll's fingertips were turned back in an affected manner, and it wore an aloof expression on its face.

He had no recollection of seeing the young man before.

"What is this?"

"It's a mannequin."

"I know that. What's it doing here?"

"I was asked to deliver it."

"You were asked? By Imura?"

"Mr. Imura, you say? No, it wasn't anybody by that name. It was Mr. Yamada."

"Yamada. . ."

"Aren't you Mr. Yamada? Didn't you order it, sir?"

"No, I didn't. And I'm not Yamada."

"You're not Mr. Yamada? This is room 6 on the fourth floor, isn't it?"

"It's not the fourth floor. This is room 6 on the third floor."

"Oh dear, I've made a mistake. Please excuse me."

The man lifted the mannequin up and carried it out into the corridor.

Mita ran up behind him, grabbed his shoulder and shook him. "Look here. You were asked to deliver it by Imura, weren't you?"

"I don't know anyone by that name. Stop shaking me! You'll break it!"

"You really don't know him?"

"Really, I don't."

The young man disappeared, and once again Mita was left alone in the room. He sat in the chair, surrounded by a feeling of suspicion. In sending the mannequin just now, wasn't Imura indicating he knew about Mita's secret room? Was it Imura that was deluding him or was he deluding himself? In any case, he now realised that in suspecting Imura, he was taking the weight off his own questionable moral self. He felt his conscience pricked yet again.

MITA NEVER CAME ACROSS Asako again in that secret room nor did she make an appearance in 'A' Bar.

Several months passed.

One day, Mita and Imura ran into each other at a bar in town, and, as they began to raise their glasses in a toast, Imura said, as if he'd suddenly remembered it, "Oh yes, when I dropped in at 'A' Bar the other day, I heard Asako had disappeared."

Silence . . .

"I heard she got married. I gather it was an arranged marriage to a steady company employee."

Silence . . .

"So, she went and married someone like that after all. Then I figured it out."

"Figured what out?"

"The reason why she flew into a rage and made that frenzied attack. This is what I think: She probably saw her own life in the appearance of those burning dolls, burning as they stood erect, their skin pouring with greasy sweat. The bar and restaurant business, well, it seems fun, but it's tough, I tell you."

"I know that," replied Mita, looking fixedly at Imura.

Mita had even more misgivings about Imura's specious conjecture. But then, what did he know about it? He felt, but was unable to say, that it was entirely possible that Asako was sitting in a secret room that Imura had somewhere in this city.

Mita fastened his eyes on Imura's face once more. But, in the end, he couldn't detect anything definite.

The Molester

―――――――――――――――――――――――――
―――――――――――――――――――――――――

I'D NEVER BEEN TO this region before, so we decided to walk through town. It was a summer afternoon, and the ground was dry and pale.

At a small post office I enquired as to the whereabouts of Tanaka Kentarō's house, and we followed the route indicated. The town was all on one side of the road, and a fence coated with coal tar ran along the right-hand side. There was a switchyard beyond the fence with a leaden railroad track. Gravel filled the gaps between the railroad ties. A long freight train, which had been making its way along at a ponderous pace, stopped just by the fence, and for a while we could hear the creaking of the train's cars and the clank of the couplers as they came into contact with one another.

Turning left, we walked in amongst the rows of houses, losing ourselves again for a while. The house we eventually located was unexpectedly humble. But there was no mistake; the sign said, 'Tanaka Kentarō, Dental Surgeon.'

The long row of tenements was located in a corner of the market. Upon opening the glass door to the entrance of one of the buildings, we found that an area adjacent to the earthen entry had been turned into an examination room. The dentist's chair on the rough, boarded floor looked like something forgotten, left behind.

It was more like a storeroom than an examination room.

"As you can see from the sign, the clinic is closed today."

A cheerless voice, it couldn't be taken as words of welcome. He'd said it perfunctorily as though it was unavoidable in fulfilling his duty. Regardless of the sign, it seemed that patients rarely visited this place.

Passing through the examination room, we came out in a four-and-a-half-mat living room. Beyond that, I could see a kitchen. There was no second floor.

Tanaka set a single white plate down on top of the low dining table, tore open a bag of buttered peanuts, turned it over and shook out the contents. With a dry sound the peanuts piled up on the plate.

He poured beer into the cups that had been placed in front of his visitors—my friend and I.

"Well now, please, go ahead," he said, in an expression of welcome.

The beer was tepid.

"I sent my wife out shopping."

"In that case, may we listen to it right away?"

A miniature tape recorder had been placed on top of the low dining table. The small, closed room was hot and muggy, and an old-fashioned electric fan whirred noisily.

"The noise from the fan is annoying, I should think."

He switched off the fan, making the room's humidity still more intense.

For a while, all we could hear was the sound of the tape recorder spools rotating, and then we began to hear the faint sound of a woman's subdued voice. It was closer to a sound than a voice, like a moan that had escaped due to the subject's distress. Yet it was mingled with a tone of delight and clearly sounded like a bedroom voice.

Though it was the first time I'd met Tanaka Kentarō, I'd corresponded with him for a long while. Twelve or thirteen years before, there had been something remarkable amongst the contributors' articles that had been sent to the amusement magazine where I was an editor.

The manuscript, entitled "The House of Maidens," described the lives of call girls in a certain provincial city, and it was both well written and highly erudite. The publication of that article in the magazine provided the opportunity, and, while corresponding with him, an image of this character Tanaka Kentarō gradually fixed itself in my imagination: a tall, good-looking man with thick eyebrows, a dark complexion, and a compact, sportsman-like physique. As the director of a dental clinic, he would be well-off too. His articles always contained something original based on information he'd paid the girls for.

Afterwards I quit my job as editor and took up writing novels, and my correspondence with him had come to an end when I left the magazine.

About ten years later, I began to serialise a work dealing with call girls in a certain weekly magazine.

It wasn't quite a novel or a documentary, nor was it a report, and it wasn't long after the serialisation had begun that a letter from Tanaka arrived in care of the editorial department of the weekly magazine. The letter set out some new information about call girls. There was a sense of nostalgia about it, and it also provided reference material for my work. Our correspondence resumed. His letters became more and more high-spirited and full of tall talk. Yet, I didn't consider them to be divorced from reality or an exaggerated, wild fancy. The things related in his letters were possible.

In one letter he wrote that if I came to that area he would introduce me to a group of prostitutes consisting of girls from good homes. So I asked a friend to go with me, and we set out for the region where Tanaka lived. My health was precarious, and I imagined the trip would be irksome, but something persuaded me to go—a letter in which he said he was on the verge of completing his research on 'sensual sounds.'

He said that in the course of his relationships with many women, he had, without their being aware of it, recorded their voices as they engaged in bedroom talk. He said he'd called the recordings 'sensual sounds' and that, based on a wealth of material, he was furthering his research into the relationships between sensual sounds and the women's appearance and their personalities.

His letter referred to 'unprecedented international research,' and while I thought it an exaggerated claim, it did hold some interest for me all the same.

I replied that I would be making the trip to see him.

By return, he sent me a single photograph of himself. A keen-eyed man with thick eyebrows stood in front of what looked like the examination room of a dental clinic, gazing into the distance. His appearance was as I had imagined it. He looked about forty, and with his deep black hair he could be said to be a handsome man. Although the photograph had been taken from a low angle showing his upper body wearing a white coat, he appeared to be fairly tall.

BUT SINCE MY ARRIVAL in this provincial city, some five hundred kilometres from my home, my image of Tanaka had begun to crumble. As he sat in front of the low dining table in the small room, I found that he was a small, thin man who had no presence about him whatsoever. I realised that he'd looked tall because of the angle of the photograph, but there was nothing of the dashing aspect of the photograph at all in the man himself. He possessed a cheerless expression and shifty eyes that flashed with paranoia now and then.

FROM THE TIME HE'D come to meet us, there was something in his manner I couldn't fathom. After passing through the ticket gate, we walked toward the waiting room, but we didn't attract the gaze of any of the men standing there. Gradually, a connection was established between those who had come to meet people and those who had arrived, and as they clapped one another on the shoulder and shook hands, we were left alone.

We looked uncertainly about us, and, as we did so, a character appeared. He was a small man wearing a mountaineer's cap and sandals on his bare feet. Assuming it was Tanaka, it didn't seem as though he was late but rather that he'd been lying low and assessing the situation from a discreet distance. He wore an ambivalent expression, and there was a look of something like fear in his eyes.

I wasn't certain it was him, so I called out to make sure.

"Mr. Tanaka?"

The doubt disappeared from his eyes, and a smile appeared on his face.

"First of all, we must have dinner," he said, his expression becoming vague once again. "I haven't booked you a hotel room. We'll listen to the tapes this evening, so I thought it would be better to stay at a hot spring resort somewhere."

"The tapes are all well and good, but I do need you to introduce us to the girls you were talking about."

"About that, as a matter of fact the police have been cracking down on that kind of thing lately, and it's gotten to the point where it would be risky to meet with the girls."

"But, they're from good homes, surely, . . ." I began to say but then realised that that was perhaps why he was so tense.

I tried rephrasing it, "But, those girls are personally acquainted with you, aren't they? Isn't there a madam's someplace where we could meet?"

"No, nothing like that."

"In that case, there's nothing to worry about even if the police are clamping down hard. No one will find fault with a personal association."

"In any case, it seems the police are keeping an eye on me. Just the other day a man who appeared to be a detective came to a house in my neighbourhood and made enquiries about me. I don't want you to get into any trouble during your trip."

His tone was intimidating. The moment I heard the timbre of his voice, I thought, *This man is lying.* It was a gut feeling, and I wasn't sure to what extent he was lying. I wondered why he wasn't telling the truth.

"In any case, let's get something to eat," I proposed, gazing again at him, with his sandals and mountaineer's cap. He reminded me of a pimp.

Perhaps he wasn't lying when he said a detective had come to make enquiries and he was misrepresenting himself as a dentist. In any case, we couldn't ask him to show us around the restaurants in town looking the way he did.

"Let's eat at a sukiyaki restaurant."

"A sukiyaki restaurant? Yes, why not. . . ."

He didn't seem to be able to think of an appropriate restaurant, so my friend, who'd been to the area twice before, led the way.

The restaurant had a tatami private room on the second floor. We ordered beef. Picking up some meat that was cooking in the pan with the tips of his chopsticks, my friend said, "It's unfortunate, isn't it? There's no longer any point to us having taken the trouble to come here."

His voice carried a reproachful ring, and I attempted to intercede, "But Mr. Tanaka, you've brought the bags with you, isn't that right? One for the tape recorder and one full of tapes. . . ."

My friend stopped eating and said meekly, "It truly is a superb collection."

In a moment the vagueness disappeared from Tanaka's face, and he took on a proud air.

"Well now, this is just part of my collection."

He placed the palm of his hand almost affectionately on the canvas bag. Then, drawing it in front of his knees, he opened the zipper. We could see small square boxes containing tapes crammed inside. Taking out one of the thin boxes, he held it in front of us. "This tape is quite something."

A piece of white paper was stuck to the lid, and on it was written data in a familiar hand.

Hanano Toriko, 23. Factory worker. Very good.

"Very good, is she? We can't tell just by looking at this. We'd like to listen to it right away," said my friend, now in a better mood.

His expression brimming with confidence, Tanaka took a small piece of paper from his pocket. "For your reference when you listen to the tapes, I'd like you to read what I've jotted down for you here."

Please note that the audio quality may have been degraded throughout the recordings. For example, the sound of a finger tapping on a table will sound like the deafening rumble of a road grader. The sound of someone blowing their nose will come across as the roar of an animal.

The fact that he'd gone to the trouble to make a note such as that seemed childish to us, and yet it made me realise just how much he was looking forward to showing off his collection.

I replied with a wry smile, partly because I'd recalled something.

"I'm sure it was just like this. It's been a few years ago now, but I once listened to a tape. We ended up trying to re-record over part of it. As it was, it was uninteresting, so we experimented by adding the sound of tissue paper in the appropriate places. We rolled the paper into a ball and made a rustling sound by the microphone. But the sound that was played back was like a paper sliding door being torn apart."

"That was a real laugh," my friend said.

Naturally, I expected Tanaka to start laughing too, but for a moment he looked put out.

"Why! In that case, have you already listened to erotic tapes before?"

"Yes, I certainly have. And, I should add, there were some phoney tapes amongst them too. There was even one where the woman was alone, but she recorded it with a tone of voice that suggested there was someone with her. . . . But you soon see through that sort of thing, don't you agree?"

"That's probably true. But it's a little unfortunate that you've already heard some."

"I don't think I will have heard anything as true to life as the tapes you have, Mr. Tanaka. Besides, seeing your article dealing with your research into sensual voices is my main objective. Do you have it with you now?"

"No. I left it at home. I'll show it to you tomorrow or some other time. By the way, about this evening—I propose we book three adjoining rooms in a hot spring hotel somewhere and get together in the middle room and listen to the tapes there. That way, we needn't be concerned about the sound being heard, and, even if it were, well, no one would find it surprising as it's that sort of place."

"In that case, Mr. Tanaka, we'd appreciate you taking us to a suitable hotel."

But he said he couldn't think of one. This too was incomprehensible. In the end, on that occasion also, we had to rely on the recollections of my friend.

Looking at my watch, I saw that it was 7:30 p.m. We arranged to meet at the hotel at 9:30. Tanaka had said he needed about an hour and a half to settle some urgent business. In the end, he failed to show up at the hotel that evening.

We tried looking him up in the telephone directory, but the number for his dental clinic wasn't listed. A clinic without a phone was inconceivable. Could he have been lying when he said he was a dentist, as I suspected? The address on the letter was that of a place on the outskirts of town. I suspected that this address too was fictitious, and so the following morning I tried sending a telegram. Copying down the telephone number of the hotel, I asked that Tanaka call me at that number.

I waited dubiously, and just as I was beginning to give up hope, the phone rang late that night. My friend answered. His voice became increasingly irritable and then exasperated.

"What about the research article on sensual sounds . . . ? What? There isn't one? Because you haven't written it yet, you say . . . ? Anyway, we at least want to listen to the tapes. Can you please come here right away by car . . . ? We said we intended to call. You said it was difficult to find a place to listen to the tapes. It was your idea to reserve rooms at this hotel, wasn't it?"

Calming my friend, I took the phone from him.

"Must I really go over there?" Tanaka's grumbling voice sounded in the receiver. I'd no idea why he had a grievance.

"In that case, I'll visit your house tomorrow," I replied.

"Alright, please do. I don't mind if you come alone if you like."

Yet again his underlying motive wasn't clear. I had no idea how to fathom his changing attitudes.

When I did locate Tanaka's house and realised he wasn't lying about being a dentist, I was even more at a loss as to what to make of him. It was a small dental clinic, without the convenience of a telephone, located in a corner of the market.

Suddenly, we heard a rumble of thunder, and a violent shower began to beat down on the tin roof. The towering midsummer clouds and the roar of thunder were refreshing, but in this small room the thunder produced a dismal, oppressive sound that only served to intensify the humidity.

It was even more difficult to catch the faint tape recording, and our three heads pressed close around the low dining table. Beads of sweat appeared on our brows. The tape that was playing was the one that bore the note 'Very good.' The sensual voice, mingled as it was with the rumble of thunder, was strangely vivid. My friend and I exchanged glances, and, I don't know why, but we nodded in tacit agreement with one another.

Noticing our behaviour, Tanaka smiled contentedly and began to comment on the tape.

The highs and lows of his rapidly changing emotions were extreme. Now in high spirits, he interspersed his explanation with gesticulations, and, slowly raising one arm, he said, "This woman, she's local. She works re-stuffing futons. She's a modest, reserved girl, and in that respect she leaves something to be desired."

The tape recorder emitted an occasional groan. Just when I thought it had gone quiet for a while, a girl's voice sounded faintly before falling silent again.

Occasionally, it was punctuated by the sound of a car horn, and from time to time we heard a man's voice. It was an indistinct voice resembling a murmur. It sounded like someone whispering sweet nothings in a woman's ear in the bedroom. The woman gradually approached climax. The intervals between her gasps became shorter, and we could distinctly hear her heavy breathing.

Sitting up straight, he said, "Any moment we'll have the climax. Very soon now. There, you see!"

In that instant, the shrill cry of a woman's voice sounded, and then it suddenly became hushed.

As he put the tape back in the box and replaced the lid, he said, "It's a little monotonous, and the tape is not entirely satisfactory."

I saw again the words 'Very good' on the white label that had been stuck to the surface of the lid.

"As a tape, it does lack something, but practically speaking it will suffice."

"That's right. A woman who is reserved like this is quite entertaining," he replied, in a calm and composed manner. Then, taking a tape from another box, he inserted it in the player. He turned the player on, and the tape began to rotate, but there was no sound. Tilting his head to one side, he looked at the label on the lid.

"Ah, I see," he murmured, "This girl didn't make a sound. All there is is a cry at the very end."

According to his tape recorder, there was about twenty minutes left before the tape came to an end. Listening to the silent tape and waiting for that cry at the end the three of us must have been an amusing sight.

"It's undoubtedly a tantalising tape, I agree. It's certainly fun waiting quietly for twenty minutes, but we don't have much time."

As I said this, we heard the honk of a car horn on the tape.

"It's the same call-girl hotel you used with the futon store worker, isn't it?"

"Eh? Why do you say that?"

"Am I wrong? I thought the sound of the horn was just as loud as the one on the tape we heard earlier."

A look of unease surfaced momentarily in his eyes, and then he looked watchful. His reaction was unexpected. I wondered why, as he began to rewind the tape.

"A scream at the very end is all well and good, but don't you have something with a little more colour?" asked my friend, his voice impatient. I could sympathise with the way he felt.

Whilst I appreciated that Tanaka actually had erotic tapes in his possession, we had not travelled several hundred kilometres to listen to recordings of this quality.

"Colourful tapes, you say? I have some of those too. Well now, here's one."

Searching through a pile of boxes, he selected one, put it in the tape player and added, by way of explanation, "As soon as I dragged this woman into the room, she went berserk. I had no choice and had to hold her down—she kicked up a real fuss."

"You dragged her into the room . . . ? Wasn't she one of the women who went to the call-girl hotel?"

"Yes, yes, that's right. I forgot to explain. While my wife was away visiting her parents, I dragged the woman back here, you see. I was surprised to find she was a virgin. Well now, listen to this."

As soon as the tape started to rotate, we heard a woman's voice, punctuated by hard breathing.

"Enough. Enough. I can't bear it any longer."

Overlaying that voice, we heard his calmer, yet muffled tones.

"Keep still."

"Ow! Ow!"

"Just a little bit more. I'm going to do it now."

"Ah, ah, ah!"

While the sobbing continued, a strange noise emanated from the tape. It was a hard sound that intermittently reverberated, a sound not unlike that produced by a hammer being used to pound in a nail.

"What's that noise?" I asked.

He replied immediately, "It's the sound of the penis entering the woman. As I told you the day before yesterday, on the tape the actual sound and the sound reproduced via the microphone are quite different. You would understand that too, I guess."

The woman's gasping voice became increasingly fervid and was interspersed with the occasional sob.

"Please, I can't stand it any longer!"

Just then, his voice was heard, "Look there! It's in right up to the root."

The car horn sounded, just as loudly as it had done on the two previous tapes.

As I began to smile wryly at his blunt language, something flashed across my mind. The muscles in my face as I tried to force a smile remained set in that position. I looked at my friend in spite of myself; there had been a change in his expression too.

With one hand I mimicked extracting a nail, so that my friend noticed what I was doing. He nodded, opened his mouth and placed his fingertip lightly against the exposed row of white teeth. It was a discreet gesture, done in such a way that Tanaka wouldn't have noticed. My friend and I silently agreed that it sounded like a dental procedure. The sound of the rain was relentless, and the interior of the room was dark and increasingly humid.

I TOOK OUT A handkerchief and hid my expression from Tanaka as I wiped the sweat from my face, wondering how to verify my suspicion. Even though I thought the recording on the tape just now was the sound of him extracting a tooth, his was a plausible story.

And, as for the woman crying out in pain and his response to 'keep still,' that would be a natural dialogue between doctor and patient. Even the frank expression 'it's in up to the root' could be interpreted to mean the needle of the hypodermic syringe was in the gum as far as the root.

But in this case it was probably safe to assume he was conscious that what he was saying was being recorded. Thinking about it that way, the meaning of 'Very good' on the label of the first box he'd shown us became clear too. It had to mean that he'd been able to make a recording that was as close to a genuinely aroused voice as possible.

As before, the tape recorder on top of the low dining table continued to exclaim, "Ow! Ow! Please stop! I can't take it any longer!"

I gazed at the machine with mixed feelings. As I did so, I became aware of something for the first time. His finger was poised above the volume control, and the moment the man's voice came on he turned the volume down. That nimble, adroit manipulation of the fingertips was the preserve of someone engaged in an occupation requiring sensitive fingertips.

It could only be interpreted as something he would do to deliberately obscure the voice for fear of it being recognized as the words of a dentist to his patient.

"Ah, ah, ah!"

A voice approaching a shriek was heard and then fell quiet.

"Finally she's achieved orgasm," he said, with an elated air.

I wasn't in the mood for losing my temper and grilling him. The tape recorder looked to me like Tanaka's pitiful plaything. There was no doubt that, for him, the tapes were not recordings of dental treatments at all but the genuine 'erotic' article. Rather than wishing to deceive us, it was clear to me that he was much more interested in deceiving himself. I suspected that while listening to the anguished voices of his female patients as they sat in the dental chair, he engaged in an idle fancy that he was locked in an embrace with them.

There was probably a microphone hidden somewhere behind the headrest. Tilting the chair all the way back, he would continue to administer treatment as he leaned over the women's bodies. He no doubt even deliberately touched their nerves with the tip of his needle in order to elicit a shriek. In his mind's eye their clothes had been removed and their bodies lay bare. Their voices were transformed into voices from the bedroom. As he concentrated on his sensitive fingers, he would become aroused, transformed.

But it suddenly occurred to me that I might be wrong. Perhaps, though seized by a violent sexual desire, his sexual organ did not in fact become aroused. I recalled his cheerless, obstinate eyes and looked about me. I had a sense of the interior of the small house—a cramped treatment room and a small living room and kitchen leading off that; that was all.

"My wife's gone shopping," he had said, but perhaps his wife too was a figment of his imagination. Perhaps he existed only within the world of those tapes. In any case, I was captivated by Tanaka's loneliness, and I wasn't annoyed at having travelled several hundred kilometres for nothing.

I had no proof, and yet I believed my own supposition to be correct. I wondered if I should return home like this, pretending to have been taken in. But would my solicitude make itself known to him?

"What gullible people writers are! They took the trouble to come all the way here, and I went and played them tapes of women having their teeth pulled. Mistaking the tapes for the real thing, they skipped home quite beside themselves with excitement."

I could almost hear him now, though of course he wouldn't actually say that to anybody. Yet I could picture him sitting alone in his room, with a wry smile, lips drawn back showing his teeth, and prattling away in a loud voice.

Hesitating for a moment, I ventured, "You're right. It was pretty raunchy, eh? But considering the woman was all worked up, it's curious that the man's voice was calm from beginning to end."

The implication was that it sounded like a doctor treating his patient, but remaining composed, Tanaka replied, "I'm getting on a bit too, you see. I manage to become aroused when I see my partner's pleasure."

"Incidentally, the tapes we've heard so far have only contained muffled sobs or voices saying things like, 'Ow!' or 'No!' Can't we listen to one where they sound like they're enjoying it?"

Silence . . .

"You know, something like, 'Yes!' or 'Hold me!' or something like that."

"Certainly. It'd be my pleasure."

He began to search through a box of tapes again. He moved with apparent confidence, and for a moment I doubted my own judgement.

But before long he stopped rummaging.

"You know, I don't have any tapes like that. . . . Women don't really say things like that."

My friend sounded impatient. "Don't be silly. Of course they do."

"Well, you might believe so, but I don't think they say things like that."

"What an absurd thing to say. . . ."

I restrained my friend, and though I felt as uncertain as before, I said in a calm, yet reproachful manner, "Mr. Tanaka, they really do say things like that."

What he said perhaps wasn't just a desperate excuse. Maybe he really didn't believe that women said such things; there was certainly something in his tone of voice that gave me that impression. His contact with women had been limited to having them sit in his chair as patients, and it seemed he'd hardly had any real experience with women. Perhaps he thought that the bedroom talk that appeared in books was all an exaggeration, bearing no resemblance to reality.

"Thank you for allowing us to listen to some unusual recordings, . . ." I said, urging my friend to stand.

The rain, which I'd thought was a summer shower, continued to fall as furiously as before.

Holding aloft a coarse oil paper umbrella, Tanaka accompanied us as far as the main street. Large drops of rain continued to pelt the paper of the umbrella, beneath which we stood side by side with him.

"Terrible rain, eh?"

"I bet it's going to pour down now," I murmured.

He turned to face me under the umbrella. A vague, uncertain expression settled on his face—as if he was wondering if his game had been perceived or whether, in fact, he'd gotten away with it.

AT THE AQUARIUM

水族館にて

At three o'clock in the afternoon, Saeki, a university student, rode the streetcar for about three minutes to the amusement park near the coast for the third day in a row. He'd set out on a whim the first two days, wearing an overcoat and gloves as it was winter, but today he had an objective in mind.

There was a small aquarium in the middle of the amusement park, and he wished to see whether today also that strange young woman would be standing there gazing into the fish tanks. The aquarium had been completely neglected, and the thick glass of the fish tanks was grimy with slime.

Bringing his eyes close to the glass and peering in at the greenish water, Saeki finally realised there wasn't a single fish in there. Elsewhere, goldfish swam around in shoals as if to apologise for the excessive number of tanks without any fish in them. Even so, they weren't an expensive variety, such as *ryūkin* or *ranchū*, but rather an inferior hybrid.

Finding the rundown aspect of the place amusing, he stood in front of the goldfish tank for a long while and gazed again at the fishless green water.

Captivated by this aquarium, he'd come to the park the past two days. He liked the cold, musty smell of the air when he set foot inside the gloomy building, the glass windows on either side of the room, and even the hazy brightness.

Perhaps he was the only one who felt that way, as the aquarium was not popular. After all, on cold days like this you wouldn't expect dozens of children and adults to come ride the merry-go-round or the miniature locomotive. In fact, there were very few people in the amusement park at all, and the aquarium was completely deserted.

Well, that wasn't entirely true. On both days, just before dusk, there had been a young woman in the building. On the first day, he'd just taken a peek at her face in profile. The next day, when he had seen the same young woman hanging around, he had passed behind her and peered into the fish tank in front of her.

There were no fish in the tank, and the thought that he'd found a kindred spirit in this woman made him smile. But even after he'd finished looking at all the fish tanks, the young woman was still standing in her original position.

"You seem to be taking your time," he murmured, fixing his gaze on her profile for a moment. The woman remained standing there, without seeming to register his presence.

THE NEXT DAY SHE was there again. Saeki looked at her with an enquiring eye for the first time. She was wearing a pair of sandals over red woollen socks. She looked as if she had just removed her apron while working in the kitchen, slipped on an overcoat and come out. He wondered if she lived in the residential area nearby the park.

"Excuse me, miss, but you must be pretty keen on fish. You come here every day."

She looked at him as though it was the first time she'd set eyes on a human being.

"I haven't come here especially because I like fish. But if you know I come here every day, you must come every day, too."

"I suppose so. I've seen you here every day, but I guess you don't remember seeing me."

"I've been wrapped up in my own thoughts. When I'm thinking about things, this sort of dimly lit space really works for me."

Then, as if the thought had suddenly occurred to her, she added, "And another thing, I'm not a 'miss,' I'm a missus."

"Oh, pardon me."

"It's alright. I don't mind. You see, even I myself don't feel like a missus yet. And yet now I've become a mother too."

"What do you mean?"

"It doesn't matter. Anyway, I've been absorbed in this and that, and I don't know why, but I find myself coming here every day."

"In that case, why don't you try heading over to the zoo to take your mind off things? They seem to look after the place a bit better than here."

Drawing in her pointy chin slightly, the woman stared at Saeki as if to ascertain who he was. The stand-up collar of his black student's uniform peeped out from his overcoat.

"You're not a delinquent university student, are you?" she said, in a light-hearted tone. "Well then, shall we go?" She set off walking. She had a light, springy step, as if she were still a student.

On the other side of the amusement park was the entrance to a small zoo. Just inside the entrance, a clapboard arcade had been erected, and pictures of various animals had been painted on the boards. They paused a while to look up at them.

"They've painted all kinds of animals up there, eh? Elephants, giraffes, lions and fur seals."

"They've got a hippo too."

"It's a small zoo, and they don't have anything very exotic in the cages, so maybe they're at least trying to drum up business with the entrance. After all, all they have in the aquarium is goldfish, right?"

"Maybe so. But, wait, there's something written beside the pictures."

A wooden board had been attached to the side of the arcade, and on it had been drawn a picture of a kangaroo. Next to that it said, 'Animals recently acquired by this zoo.'

— 29 —

That picture alone had been freshly painted while the others were rather faded.

Saeki looked suspiciously around the arcade.

"Can there really be so many different kinds of animals in such a small space as this? It would make it as good as Ueno Zoo, don't you think? It's hard to believe, if you ask me."

"Anyhow, shall we go in?"

This time, the woman eagerly pulled him by the arm.

When they went inside, all the animals portrayed in the pictures were there.

But there were so many unusual animals crammed into that small space that they really didn't have much room at all. And there was only one elephant, one giraffe and one hippo. The hippo was lying down as if it had been packed in a box in the middle of its small, heated room in such a way that it couldn't move an inch. Only its head stuck out above the water tank.

"It's true. They really are all here, aren't they? But they can't be happy crammed together like this. The conditions are much better in the aquarium. That hippo—looks like a guy suffering from a hangover with his head stuck in the sink."

The woman laughed cheerfully at his remark.

In making a complete circuit of the zoo, her mood brightened, and she began to treat Saeki as a friend. Even when she saw the signboard in front of the lion's enclosure, which read 'Warning: liable to urinate if you come too close,' she was able to say in a carefree voice, "Oh! What a vulgar lion he is!"

Not wishing to let the opportunity slip, he thought he'd try asking her what sort of things had been on her mind. The anxieties of a woman who stood facing an empty fish tank every day—they had to be something unusual.

Night falls early in winter, and at half past four a bell sounded a long ring, indicating the zoo was closing. As if hurried along by the peal of the bell, they walked shoulder to shoulder along the soft, sandy path. The woman began gradually to answer his questions.

"When I pick the baby up, the skin on my arms becomes red and swollen where it touches him. Then when I put him down, before long, the swelling goes right down again."

"Wait a minute. You say your arms swell up? And it's because of the baby? What baby?"

"About two months ago, a baby burst into my life. Of course, I gave birth to him, but for some reason or other I had the feeling that a stork had carried him there in its bill."

She began to tell her story. About a year before she'd married a company employee who was about ten years her senior. She wasn't sure why, but her parents were very keen to marry her off just as soon as she'd graduated high school.

Even the plans she'd made herself were, in the end, crushed by her parent's ardour, and she married a man she neither liked nor disliked. He was fond of her and devoted himself to his young wife, whose energy and zest for life reminded him of a student. She gradually became accustomed to married life, and yet the ambivalent feelings she had for her husband remained unchanged.

She conceived right away, and though she thought it too soon to bear a child, her husband strongly urged her to have it. Perhaps, perceiving his wife's equivocal feelings toward him, he thought that having a child would allay her sense of insecurity.

On this occasion too, she withdrew into herself, and before long the baby was born.

"And when I picked the baby up, my arms swelled up, you see."

"Something somehow happens with the nerve endings under the skin where you touch the baby, don't you think? Maybe it causes a temporary inflammation. They say that in ancient times when martyrs thought hard about Christ, a red crucifix would appear on their skin. That was probably a symptom similar to yours. So the moment you pick your baby up, you must be experiencing strong emotions about something. The fact that it affects your skin means you have a 'predisposition to allergies,' to use a popular phrase."

"You say I must be experiencing strong thoughts about something, but what sort of things, I wonder. Maybe you're right. So it's because every day I stand in the gloom in the aquarium absentmindedly lost in thought. Is that what you mean?"

"Anyhow, who's looking after your baby now?"

"I locked the house and came out while he was taking his midday nap. So, he's probably crying in the house about now."

"You don't hate your baby, do you?"

Silence . . .

"You're saying the baby is something uninvited that has intruded on the life you have with your husband?"

"Maybe it's because when I pick him up my arms swell up. And when I put him down, they get better right away. Maybe my husband's an intruder who burst into my life too. I had a dream about doing a job which would allow me to be independent. I can't tell you what kind of job it is as I get embarrassed when I'm laughed at. I regret not making that dream come true. I don't mean to hate my husband."

The path meandered through the woods. Houses—some with red roofs, some with tiled roofs—were dotted here and there amongst the trees. The surrounding scenery slowly passed by as the couple walked along the sandy ground at a leisurely pace, preoccupied by their conversation.

When the woman drew near the edge of the path and stood in front of the entrance to a Western-style house, Saeki mechanically followed. Turning around, she began to gesture slightly to him, but as he was already standing right behind her she turned to face the door again.

As she stooped and fumbled noisily for the keyhole with the key she'd taken out of her pocket, suddenly the porch light came on.

The twilight hues glared into colour in the light from the electric bulb. In the next instant, the door opened from the inside.

Saeki found himself facing a man, with the woman in between them. Needless to say, the short, stoutly built man was her husband.

"Oh! You're home early today."

"I came home the same time I always do. The house was dark and the baby was crying. That's not very good really, is it?"

In a voice suggesting he was suppressing his feelings, the man spoke civilly, as if he were admonishing a child, and his tone sounded doleful. Still leaning out from the doorway, he studied Saeki's face, and said, "And who is this boy?"

"He's a gentleman I met for the first time a little while earlier just over there. He's a medical student. We were just walking this way, and I was asking his advice about the swelling on my arm."

As a result of this awkward lie, Saeki began to form the impression that something intimate had developed between him and the woman.

"So, that's what you do, is it—confide that sort of thing in a complete stranger? Well now, that's just fine. You can tell me all about it later."

Turning toward Saeki, he said in a formal tone of voice, "Hurry on home, will you? It's not every day you open your door to find some stranger standing pressed up close behind your wife."

"I didn't mean to come to your home at all. I'm new to this area, and before I knew it I found myself standing here face-to-face with you."

"Are you saying it would have been better to have gone home without having been seen by me?"

"There's nothing particularly suspicious about it, I assure you. The way your wife explained it is pretty much how it is. I don't even know her name."

"Her name is Hisako. But that's all the same to you. You're a confounding man. Hurry up and go home, will you?"

The young man in front of him made her husband suspicious, and his voice took on an impatient tone, suggesting he was afraid something unexpected was about to unfold.

"Well then, how can I get to the street with the trams? I've only just arrived here and landed at my relative's home, so I don't know my way round."

"Is that right? You've only just come to town? It's quite a winding road to get to the tram street."

"In any case, can you help me out? I can't very well have your wife escort me there, so please either take me there yourself or draw me a map."

Saeki persisted, deliberately, as a means of venting his annoyance at being suspected when in fact he was innocent. The man opened and closed his mouth two or three times, then said, "You must be kidding. Find your own way back."

Then the door slammed shut in Saeki's face, like a shell closing its lid.

SAEKI WASN'T LYING WHEN he'd said he was a stranger to those parts. He'd arranged to stay at his relative's house, which was in a quiet neighbourhood, in order to finish his graduation thesis. But the way things were going, it didn't look as though he would make any progress.

The following day too, he began to grow restless when it turned 3 o'clock. He'd become accustomed to going out at that time. Putting his coat on and going outside, he found that his feet naturally carried him in the direction of the amusement park.

There was no sign of the woman that day. Saeki pressed his forehead against the glass and peered in at the green water in the tanks. As he did so, a scorpion fish swam unsteadily out from between the rocks at the back of one of the tanks that until the day before he was sure contained no fish.

It swam right over to the other side of the glass and then rotated its protruding eyes round and round in front of Saeki.

'You can wait all you like, but it doesn't look as though anyone's coming.'

He suddenly felt as though this small fish was ridiculing him. And yet at three o'clock the next day, and the day after that too, he left the house in order to visit the aquarium. Whilst it appeared that he was stubbornly repeating the same routine, he also felt sure that the woman would come to the aquarium one more time.

Sure enough, on the fourth day, the sound of sandals slapping against the concrete floor of the aquarium resounded through the building quickly reaching his ears.

"Oh! I didn't think I'd bump into you again here."

"Well, I did."

"I'm really sorry about what happened the other day. My husband was rude to you, wasn't he? In the state I was in, I was only able to say something half-hearted. It would have been much better if you'd been out and out angry with me."

"I was afraid you'd run away. That's why I wasn't."

"That's the sort of person you are, I suppose. But, I'm glad we were able to see each other again. There's something I'd like to tell you."

"I'm not a medical student, you know. But I thought I might be able to see you here, and so I've been waiting."

"You've been waiting for me?"

"I don't really know if I've been waiting for you, or waiting to find out how your arms are."

"That's what I want to tell you about," said the woman, beginning to explain.

That night, her husband had again demanded an explanation for her behaviour that day. This time, she'd given him a coherent account of what really happened: that a university student had struck up a conversation with her as she stood lost in thought in the dimly lit aquarium.

Little by little, a careless tone had begun to find its way into her explanation as if to suggest she didn't care whether or not he believed her. A look of bafflement had lingered in his expression, but he hadn't pressed the matter further.

The following day he hired a housekeeper. He said it would free her from having to look after the baby, but no doubt that wasn't the only reason. Her husband's manner became increasingly obliging. Almost every night on his return from work, he would take her out for some recreation or other. He took her to dinner at the restaurant in a hotel on a hill overlooking the sea and accompanied her to a first-run movie.

The night before, he had invited her out to a cabaret.

The hostesses at what seemed to be his favourite bar when on company business paid him compliments.

"Well now, this gentleman has a wife to be proud of. She really is pretty, isn't she?"

"She really is a sweetie, not like a wife at all."

She found her husband's notion that she would be cheered up by such words, unpleasant. Coming to a man's place of amusement, it pained her to see her husband allowing the girls who worked there lavish such praise on her. She found the sheer nerve of her husband taking her there disagreeable.

By and by, her husband lured her out onto the floor and they began to dance. He tried a variety of difficult and intricate steps on the small dance floor, which also succeeded in offending her. Every aspect of her husband's behaviour that evening ran counter to her mood.

While she was dancing, she suddenly felt there was something wrong with the arm she had around her husband's back. It was exactly the same sensation she'd experienced when she had held the baby in her arms. She knew, even without baring her arm, that it was red and swollen.

Having a high opinion of his own dancing, her husband continued to dance with her to several more melodies. She endured the uncomfortable sensation in her arm without complaint.

After a number of melodies, her husband finally let her go. They sat down in their original booth, and after a short while the pain in her arm abated like an ebbing tide.

"I THOUGHT ABOUT WHAT you said the other day, and I think what I just told you proves that in my heart I hate my husband."

For some reason, Saeki felt a little flustered and changed the subject.

"I'd like just once to see that swelling on your arm. My winter vacation will soon be coming to an end. . . ."

"In that case, why not come back with me to my house, like you did the other day? I'll show you what happens when I pick up the baby."

"I can't do that. Your husband will start yelling that a strange guy has been in his house again without him knowing."

The bell began to sound indicating that the park was closing for the day. Exchanging glances, they walked side by side along the sandy path in the wood toward the park gates. There wasn't a soul to be seen.

"As I said, I won't be going to your house," said Saeki, abruptly.

She came to a halt and looked him in the eye.

Then, raising both arms slowly, she quietly slipped them around his waist. Embracing his body within the ring formed by her arms, she clasped her hands together and slowly squeezed him.

"There's nothing the matter with my arms when I put them around you," she whispered in his ear.

The next instant she gave out a cry and suddenly withdrew her arms. She put them behind her back, clearly trying to conceal them from him.

"What's the matter?"

"Something's wrong. My arms feel strange."

Raising her arm, he quickly rolled up her sleeve. Dusk was drawing near, but even in the dim light he could see that her arm was red and swollen. She snatched her arm back from his grip and hid it under her clothing. "It's not right, I tell you. There's no reason why I would hate you," she said. "Do you understand? It's not right, I tell you. I get it. That must be it. When my mood swings violently, my arm swells up like this, do you see? I don't need you to explain it to me. Yes, that must be it."

Saeki was disturbed by what he heard. He studied something that moved violently about within himself.

It seemed to him as though everything was going to collapse and take an unexpected direction. In marshalling his thoughts, he deliberately took time to ask himself one question: *What have I been waiting for these last few days in the semidarkness of that aquarium? This woman? Or was it in order to find out about the condition of those abnormal arms?*

He took a cigarette out of his pocket and lit it. Before long, he was able to speak calmly.

"That's right. It's just as you say. It seems the allergic reaction occurs when your nerves are excessively stimulated."

The silence continued for a while.

Then, in an eager, yet affectionate tone of voice, he said, "The other day, you were talking about doing a job which would allow you to stand on your own two feet, remember? You said you were embarrassed and wouldn't tell me what you did. Won't you tell me now?"

Without saying anything, she reached out and plucked the cigarette from between Saeki's fingers.

She brought the cigarette to her lips and drew deeply on it. Then, she replied simply, exhaling smoke as she did so.

"I painted pictures."

Putting the cigarette to her lips again, she took a drag. As she inhaled, smoke went into one of her eyes. Though it had grown dark, for some reason the image of that one eye—open wide and misty—lingered vividly in his mind.

Treatment

治療

LYING IN THE ROOM, I gazed absentmindedly at the Easter lilies arranged in the vase on top of the chest of drawers. Each time the lilies breathed, their heads—with petals stuck to one another they resembled old-fashioned gramophone horns, emitted a cloud of microscopic yellow pollen which seemed to fill the room and gave me trouble breathing.

I was taking time off work during the typhoon season. We had been repeatedly battered by storms, some large and some not so large, and I had sensed I would succumb to an asthma attack. My whole being seemed to have become a precisely calibrated measuring instrument, the tips of its various needles quivering in response to subtle changes in atmospheric pressure and temperature. There's a type of asthma attack triggered by the pollen of particular kinds of flowers. In extreme cases, once the symptoms develop, just setting eyes on artificial flowers of that kind and smelling their imaginary fragrance is enough to bring on a seizure.

As I was gazing at the lilies, I recalled a story I'd heard a few days before.

I had heard that a friend invariably suffered an asthma attack whenever he ate things like prawns. In my own case, I have trouble with changes in the seasons or atmospheric pressure. While it's not my intention to discuss allergies, if I were to cite an even more peculiar example, I know a man who suffered an asthma attack while gazing at an oil painting by Picasso depicting a deformed human face with nine nostrils. I burst out laughing imagining his nearly six-foot burly frame bent double with the difficulty of breathing in front of Picasso's cubist picture in the Bridgestone Museum of Art. (Quite a number of people mistakenly believe that asthma is an old person's affliction, but as you can gather from examples such as these, the illness relates to the nervous system and has nothing to do with age.)

As chance would have it, my wife learned of a skilled physician who had a cure for asthma. Actually, these days it seems there are a surprising number of people suffering from this ailment, and in the worst of the seasons sometimes asthma is all people ever seem to talk about.

But the tale my wife had heard from an elderly woman in the neighbourhood was pretty odd to say the least. Far from recommending him, the woman seemed to have beaten a hasty retreat from the doctor's surgery.

According to my wife, the elderly woman had described the events as follows:

"I heard he could cure even the most serious types of asthma. So I went along for a medical examination. And what do you suppose happened? Well, I'll tell you. He came into the examination room carrying a beat-up old charred pan together with a syringe he'd been boiling. Well, I know a thing or two about disinfection, and so I excused myself sharpish and went home right away." Then she added, "He really is a moody man. What with that sour expression of his—as if he was smiling at something that had just occurred to him. It was a fearful sight. Just like a devil he was."

I liked the sound of the doctor in that story; I could perceive from amongst the matters she described so distastefully the type of character who was absorbed in the pursuit of a single aim. Characters I was on friendly terms with—the stubborn master carpenter, the barber, the dry cleaner—became fused with the image of the doctor and danced about in my imagination.

The following day I went right away to the doctor's surgery. Though I'd set out feeling extremely well-disposed towards him, this fifty-something doctor, by contrast, was in a foul mood. He was unsmiling throughout. If anything, it might have been more apt to describe his facial expression as *disinterested*.

"Your asthma is what we might call 'beginner' level," he told me.

No matter how much I protested the severity of my attacks and even when I complained about the agony I was in whenever I had to run for any sustained period, gasping for breath, my ephedrine and adrenaline injections no longer having any effect, he simply repeated the same thing over and over again. Be that as it may, for several months afterwards I went to his surgery every Sunday for treatment. Though it was a straightforward procedure whereby the doctor would extract blood from my vein into a syringe before injecting it once again subcutaneously, it seemed that a fine attention to detail was required when it came to considerations such as the volume of blood to be used.

Though I went to the highly regarded Dr. Yamamoto's surgery for treatment on many occasions, his disinterested expression was always the same. While visiting his surgery I realised that his mood seesawed according to the condition of the patients who came to see him.

On one particular Sunday morning, I was undergoing an examination, having stripped to the waist and bared my chest. Just then the door opened, and a patient who was suffering a violent spasm was brought through. Seeing the patient, the doctor's face became suddenly animated and, having been abandoned, I was left looking on at the frenetic pace of activity.

Firstly, he sucked clear liquid from an ampoule into an extremely fine syringe with a glass tube coated purple on the inside, held it up and checked the amount of the drug before injecting it into the patient's upper arm. Next, he inserted a glass tube with a long, rubber pipe fixed to one end into the patient's mouth, squeezed and then suddenly released the rubber ball that was attached to the other end and atomized the liquid medicine into the patient's throat.

Then, handing him a metal basin, he berated his gasping patient while beating against his heaving back. "Look here, you'll have to cough harder and bring up the phlegm. Go on, go on!"

Although in point of fact these treatments required a fair amount of time to carry out, they seemed to me to have been performed one after another with dizzying speed. This was no doubt due to the powerful vitality that played about the doctor's person and punctuated each and every one of his actions.

As if he'd finally remembered I was there, in the middle of a feeling of excitement which refused completely to abate the doctor waved his arms about in broad gestures and turned to my already naked form, ordering, "Ah, now then, you, hurry up and take your shirt off. Come on, hurry now."

Thus, the asthma which to me was a heavy burden, was, as far as the doctor was concerned, of no value; it followed, therefore, that I was nothing more than a completely worthless man whose presence in the examination room aroused no interest whatsoever in Dr. Yamamoto. Although I convinced myself that it was generally desirable that nothing superfluous lingered in the relationship between doctor and patient, his moody, sour expression made me feel ill at ease.

Then one day I appeared before him, saddled with my 'unworthy' asthma, and, in an attempt to give myself more gravitas than I actually had (the proverb 'an ass in lion's skin' coming to mind), I tried broaching the subject of my friend.

"One of my friends has an asthma attack the moment he eats shellfish like prawns. What do you suppose causes that?"

As I spoke, the doctor's usually sullen face abruptly began to brighten.

"Really? Well now, would you mind introducing your friend to me?"

It was an unprecedentedly gentle voice, resonating the sort of petulant tone a child would use in pestering its mother for a toy. On my way home I couldn't stop smiling as I recalled the change in the doctor's expression and the words he'd spoken at that moment.

BEFORE I REALISED IT a week had gone by and it was once again time for me to go in for my treatment. As I went into the examination room, the doctor beamed, greeting me with a nod; then, looking away, his expression unchanged, he fixed his gaze on the entrance. It was then that I suddenly realised what the matter was. He'd been expecting me to be accompanied by my friend with the prawn-induced asthma attacks.

It was rather like visiting an old man who loves pickled horseradish empty-handed to report on a trip to Shizuoka.

Sure enough, an unmistakable look of disappointment appeared on the doctor's face. And while it didn't readily dissipate, neither did he voice his feelings. Afterwards, he was much friendlier than he usually was, so I resolved that by the following Sunday I would visit my friend and at least find out his intentions.

But I was overcome by a feeling of lethargy—his house being in the far reaches of the suburbs, and a week went by without my having done anything. Feeling beholden to the doctor, and in an effort to keep things on an even footing, I was conscious I'd gone into the examination room wearing a stern expression. The treatment came to an end, and I was on the point of leaving for home without having said anything; I wished to bring an end to this irksome matter. Without taking his eyes off me, the doctor was curiously hesitant. Then, at length, he said, "I was wondering whether you'd managed to speak with the friend you mentioned the other day with the prawn problem?"

I replied, with an expression that suggested it was the first time I'd given it any thought, "Ah, him. I haven't had a chance to see him recently, I'm afraid."

"Really? Well then, when you do meet him next, please tell him that I can make him better so that he will be able to eat prawns."

In the end, I found myself compelled to pay a visit to my friend.

One evening, on my way home from work, I eventually arrived at his house, having changed trains three times. Explaining the course of events so far, I implored him to accompany me just once for treatment by this eminent physician. He chuckled and gave a slight shake of the head as if he thought it amusing, though he did seem kindly disposed towards the doctor.

But his parting words were, "I'm absolutely fine so long as I don't eat prawns. Besides, it's not as if I'm particularly fond of them. Well now, why not refuse him with a joke or something? You know, maybe tell him I'd eat it for him if he buys me a delicious meal."

His reluctance was perfectly understandable; after all, no one in their right mind wants to be used as a guinea pig for some experiment. But the doctor took it the wrong way.

"He was pretty selfish and said something like if you treat him to a splendid meal he might be willing to do it, but. . . ."

As I began to explain, the doctor, all smiles, said, "Ah, that's no problem. I'll treat him to a marvellously large lobster." Then, suddenly lowering his voice as if he were confiding some grave secret to me, he whispered in my ear, "As a matter of fact, your kind of asthma is really commonplace, but it's pretty unusual to come across someone who suffers an attack when they eat prawns. His is a rare case, you realise."

I brought to mind a deep red, spiny lobster, its long, sharp feelers extended to their fullest and ten legs splayed out and firmly planted on top of a white plate. I was especially partial to shellfish like prawns and crab. But at that moment the form of the lobster seemed detestable to me.

The following Sunday I skipped my appointment. Around that time, the treatment had begun to take effect, and since I was hardly ever bothered by spasms any more, I stopped going to the sessions.

I tried making one more visit to my friend's place intent on persuading him to change his mind. Travelling via the three stations wasn't easy. At one station, I had to wait a long time for a train, and at another the electrically-operated doors of the train shut right in front of me and I had to watch a long line of cars slowly start moving away.

With a sense of irritation, I wondered why I felt compelled to go on this foolish errand. How had it all started? Perhaps from the embarrassment of finding that my asthma was nothing out of the ordinary. Then I'd broached the subject of my friend and his reaction to eating prawns in order to divert Dr. Yamamoto's attention from that very ordinariness. As a consequence, I was running around like this eager to please the doctor by attempting to persuade my friend to see him.

I felt unable to break the doctor's enduring fixation with my friend. I wondered whether I was attempting to sacrifice myself for the advancement of medical science. Or perhaps I was simply trying to satisfy the doctor's curiosity. Come to think of it, wasn't Dr. Yamamoto's personality, that personality I'd felt warmly drawn to and which was at the root of all of this, now beginning to get to me?

I'd tried to win my friend over somehow or other and take him along to the doctor's. I seemed to be trying to wear him down in much the same way the doctor was grinding me down, notwithstanding my friend's stubborn resistance.

"I must admit, I like the sound of this Dr. Yamamoto. But why on earth must I eat a large lobster in front of a complete stranger simply to demonstrate I suffer from asthma? It's not as if you don't know how painful the attacks are."

"You want to know why? The advancement of medical science, that's why."

"But I don't have a sense of self-sacrifice."

"In any case, what do you say? You'll be able to eat prawns without a care in the world."

"How many times do I have to spell it out for you? I don't like prawns."

"But not ever being able to eat them means you'll be missing something in life."

"I've never heard such ridiculous logic."

We exchanged a variety of other strange snatches of conversation of the sort that, had I been a bystander listening in, would have had me in stitches. Nevertheless, we were both in earnest, and, at length, vexed with one another we fell into a sulky silence.

Before I realized it, it was late. With nothing else for it, I decided to stay and had some bedding laid out next to my friend. I'd already given up on him. But I fell asleep resolving that, when morning came, I would try to entice him one more time.

At daybreak I was awakened by my friend repeating the same thing over and over in clear tones, "Laquelle the lobster is coming to get me. Laquelle the lobster is coming."

Looking at his face as he repeated this, it occurred to me that, though he was shouting the words quite distinctly, he was in fact talking in his sleep. Before long, he started to emit a hoarse sound from the back of his throat—the precursor to an asthma attack. I considered shaking him awake if it seemed the spasms were going to worsen, but after a short while the creaking in his bronchial tubes ceased, and he began to breathe normally again.

A lobster by the name of Laquelle. . . . I realised *laquelle* was a feminine interrogative pronoun in the French language that means 'which.' The words my friend had shouted didn't have any particular meaning but were probably the result of a chance combination of sounds. Only I was sure that in his dream he'd screamed that he was being pursued by a giant lobster with its deep red feelers raised in the air. Now that I thought about it, there was a Spanish actress called Raquel Meller. She was a star of silent movies, and one of the passionate roles she had played was Carmen.

When sunlight filled the room I asked my friend, who by now was awake, "Did you have a bad dream last night?"

"No. I slept well. Why? Is something the matter?"

I'd no reason to think he was lying. But then, neither did I doubt that a terrifying nightmare had passed like a phantom without trace through the recesses of his mind. At the same moment I realised the urge to have him see Dr. Yamamoto had also evaporated.

I didn't mention a word about the prawns, so while eating breakfast he offered some casual observations about that oppressive subject which had occupied our thoughts since the night before.

"I'm sorry I can't help you. Please forgive me. Instead let me tell you about something that happened a long while back, which portended my being unable to eat prawns. It was when I was a kid. I was trying to shell a prawn, and some juice spurted into my eye. Right away half of my face swelled up horribly. It turned out to be a bad case of hives. As I'd suspected all along, there's a link between asthma and skin ailments," he said. "Oh, and another thing, did you hear about S's son having mild asthma when he eats meat? When I saw S the other day, he told me about it. He said he was at his wits' end."

When it was time for my next treatment instead of taking my friend with me I told the doctor the good news about S's son.

"I'm sorry to say that my friend won't agree to come with me, but I do have another friend whose son has an asthma attack when he eats meat."

The doctor's eyebrows twitched spasmodically and his eyes gleamed. "Oh, really? And how old would you say the child is?"

More so than prawns, it must have been quite an inconvenience to be unable to eat meat; it would probably be far easier to take S's son along to see the doctor. And in doing so, I would have discharged my responsibility, I reflected, as I made my reply. "About five I should think."

The doctor looked suddenly crestfallen. "That won't do. Unless he's at least elementary school age, there's no way of treating him." Having spoken so conclusively, he lapsed into silence for a while. Before long, he unexpectedly began to chuckle. "I would much prefer to meet your friend with the prawn allergy, if you don't mind," he rasped, peering at me, his voice like a whisper.

In that instant, his grinning face looked to me for the first time like the devil the old woman had talked about.

I felt practically a physiological pain when I imagined the following Sunday and the moment when, all alone, I would turn the doorknob to the doctor's examination room.

One evening around that time, having had an unexpected windfall, my wife and I were eating out at a small Western-style restaurant in town.

"I'll have prawns au gratin. Naturally, you'll have the same, won't you?"

Knowing that prawns were my favourite dish, my wife gave her order to the waitress, who was standing nearby. As she did so, I had a vision of Dr. Yamamoto's smiling countenance, and a feeling of aversion for this strange-shaped crustacean welled up within me.

"No. I think I'll give the prawns a miss."

I was on the point of taking up the menu, when the waitress interrupted, "We can't prepare the au gratin unless it's for a minimum of two servings."

"Really? In that case, I'll have the same," I said, looking up at her. A loathsome expression must have surfaced on my face, as if I thought *she* was a lobster or something.

The prawns were delicious after all. I ate every bit, right into the corners of the scallop-shaped dish. Just then, something strange happened. As we were drinking our after-dinner coffee, my wife, who was sitting opposite me peered into my face, tilting her head to one side.

"Your face looks kind of strange."

Now that she mentioned it, I had been feeling uncomfortable all over for a little while. Conscious of the people round about in the brightly lit room, I borrowed my wife's pocket mirror and looked at my reflection. Peering into the mirror, I could see that my eyelids, the sides of my nose and the skin around my cheekbones were swollen and angry. In a moment, my eyelids puffed up and began to cover my eyes. Flustered, I urged my wife outside, where we hailed a cab and returned home. Soon after, something resembling eczema began to appear on the skin around my neck too.

The skin elsewhere remained as it normally was. There wasn't much of an itching sensation either. But an oppressive feeling bore down on me, as though the condition had spread throughout my entire body, almost as though my cutaneous respiration had somehow been impeded. As an attempt at self-help, I tried applying a nettle rash medicine, but it had no effect whatsoever. Yet, I was convinced it was a type of nettle rash. I wondered whether nettle rash and asthma didn't share the same symptoms.

The general discomfort I was experiencing intensified. I could picture the inflamed lining of my stomach, several metres of intestinal wall, and the insides of all manner of blood vessels. At the same time, I experienced a feeling of great relief rising up from the bottom of that feeling of discomfort. For the first time I was confident I would be able to visit the doctor with nothing to be ashamed of. Opening the door, I would march into the examination room and, even though Dr. Yamamoto was bound to look beyond me for another, I would no longer feel ashamed. My friend with the prawn problem, who ought to have been following on behind me, had become internalised within me, and it was I who would send the doctor into raptures of delight; I experienced an emotion close to joy.

But as that feeling left me, like the ebbing of the tide, this time a different thought came to mind: why had this phenomenon visited itself on me? The doctor's persistent heckling having finally eroded my self-confidence, could my friend's condition have migrated into the vacuum thus created? I wondered whether I would ultimately give in to the doctor's requests.

The following morning, though my skin had greatly recovered, patches of angry-looking swelling remained.

Although it wasn't my day for treatment, I set out at once for the doctor's. As before, two opposing feelings resided within me, but I felt a sense of delight when I imagined the doctor's smiling face. That face, at that moment, was not at all like the devil.

I flung open the door of the examination room. "Look what happened when I ate prawns. Please. Can't you do something for me?"

My voice was shriller than usual, and conscious of its wheedling tone I felt disgusted with myself. Nonetheless, my expectations in relation to the doctor's reply were so great that such feelings were immediately swept away.

But I felt utterly betrayed. Casting a glance at my face, he said, his tone practically indifferent, "Oh, it's a little swollen, eh?"

The expression in his eyes as he turned his gaze on my skin was exactly as it had been when he'd looked askance at my undistinguished asthma.

Feeling insulted, I said acerbically, "It swelled up less than ten minutes after I ate prawns. Just as I thought, it's a type of allergy."

Glancing at me with a sullen look, the doctor said, "The trouble is these days people attribute anything and everything to allergies. Things have come to a pretty pass. It's just a straightforward skin disease, that's all."

Springing to his feet, he took down a small, slender glass bottle from the drug shelf and handed it to me. "Try applying this."

I reached out in spite of myself and took the small bottle. Gazing at the yellow liquid pitching about inside, I suddenly felt ablaze with a sense of shame. "So, are you saying it has nothing to do with the prawns?"

"I think it's simply a coincidence."

"But my friend told me that when he got prawn juice in his eye his face swelled right up."

"That's different from asthma."

The doctor's tone revealed a sense of obstinacy and cool logic in asserting his own theories. So I resisted the urge to say what I really wanted to say: *In that case, have you no intention of treating my prawn-induced nettle rash?* Had I said as much, the doctor was bound to have pointed to the glass bottle in my hand and replied, without so much as raising an eyebrow, "Apply that medicine, why don't you?"

Seeing me lapse into silence, he began to lecture me in a deliberate, high-handed manner. "According to current theories, it would seem that asthma is brought on when the nerves around the bronchial tubes go into convulsion, compressing the tubes and causing difficulty in breathing. But my own theory is that it's caused by phlegm collecting in the bronchial tubes. Consequently, in order to treat asthma, I believe it is necessary to eliminate this phlegm. Yesterday some people from 'A' Newspaper came by to hear my views, and they took photographs too." At this point, and without affectation, the doctor's face crumpled delightedly. "They're going to turn it into an article in the near future, and when they do I'd like you to read it carefully."

Realising that all the while I'd been holding the bottle with the yellow liquid tightly in my grasp, I became annoyed and thrust it into my pocket. Then, half in a rage, I stormed out of the examination room.

I'D NO INTENTION WHATEVER of using that yellow drug, although it seemed my skin disease would never clear up. Generally, allergy symptoms clear up remarkably quickly after some time has elapsed, but my symptoms persisted for a long while. In the end, wearied by the symptoms, I fancied I'd try the medicine Dr. Yamamoto had given to me. Taking out the cork stopper, I poured a few drops of the liquid, experimentally, on my fingertip; it had a glutinous feel, and a strong pungent smell tickled my nose. I tried dabbing a small amount on my face, but it was no good. Irritated by the liquid, my skin swelled up angrily once again. Before long, my eyelids began to close, and my skin relapsed to the worst of conditions.

Yet I can't deny that I didn't entertain a private hope that the doctor's medicine would have no effect and produce such disappointing results.

About a week passed, and my ailment finally cleared up on its own. Since then, I've avoided eating prawns. I was afraid that eating them would cause my skin to become inflamed again. But, at the same time, I was also afraid it wouldn't elicit any reaction at all; I was at a complete loss.

One day, while I was in a restaurant in town, thinking nothing of it I ordered Chinese noodles. Looking at the bowl the waiter had brought out I could see two or three small prawns floating in the broth. After a moment's hesitation, I picked the prawns out of the bowl one by one with my chopsticks and then consumed the noodles. But about an hour later, the same symptoms, though not as pronounced as before, appeared once again on the skin above my neck. In my opinion, it was because the extract from the prawns had been mixed in with the broth, though, of course, Dr. Yamamoto's view would no doubt have been that it was unrelated and simply a 'skin disease.'

Until recently, I'd laughed away the story of my friend and his prawn 'allergy.' But now, whenever I had to buy a meal in town, my order would be followed by some hitherto unnecessary cautionary comment such as, "There's no prawn in the chilled noodles, right?" or, "I'll have the rice and steamed vegetables. Only, don't put any prawns in it."

Ever since that minor incident, my skin had become all the more sensitive. Walking around town, I noticed restaurant display windows featuring plates of spiny lobster, their backs split lengthways to reveal white flesh striped with reddish brown, the scattered black spots on the shell that had been boiled a deep red, its two long feelers covered all over with fine, stiff hair, and its ten legs. When I caught sight of this, I felt something squirming to the surface from deep within myself, the sensation playing just below my skin.

Had I lingered much longer I knew that I'd be forced to witness the skin from my neck upwards—reflected dully in the show window glass—gradually swell up and turn red. So I quickly left. Choosing back streets where it didn't appear there were any restaurants, I followed a zigzag course through the town. But on this particular occasion, unfortunately another restaurant barred my way in an intimidating manner.

Each time I ventured into town, I felt I knew just how a criminal on the run must feel, though of course that was probably a slight exaggeration. In any case, before long I was exasperated with my own timid behaviour.

Notwithstanding Dr. Yamamoto's protestations, I was sure that it was my nervous predisposition that triggered the dermatitis when I ate prawns. Yet until recently I had been able to eat them with no difficulty at all. It followed, therefore, that I ought to be able to eat prawns again within a short period of time.

One Sunday evening, a fortnight after I'd stopped going to the doctor's, I stuffed several 100 yen notes into my pocket and set out for a restaurant. I plumped down in a seat and, bracing myself, gave my order in a grave tone of voice.

"Give me the cold lobster."

With a gleaming silver knife and fork held at the ready, I fell to on the lobster, which was still in its shell on the large plate that had been brought out before long. Tearing the meat from the shell, I popped strips of it into my mouth and chewed unhurriedly. Though it was tender, it had a resilience that pressed back against my teeth, and the sensation of it going down my throat seemed to last forever. I was pitted in a battle. But who, I wondered, was my adversary? Was it the lobster? Or was it Dr. Yamamoto? Perhaps it was myself.

After I'd eaten all of it, I waited two or three minutes before lightly stroking a finger across my face. Nothing happened at all. Slowly rising from my seat, I left the restaurant. I walked along in a leisurely manner, losing myself amongst the early evening crowds.

The sky was aglow with the sunset, and wispy clouds appeared near the horizon. The city skyline was unevenly delineated by buildings of various sizes, the dome-shaped roof of a church standing out conspicuously. I felt exhilarated. Wasn't it true that there was nothing the matter with my skin? I took a deep breath. And in that instant yet again I felt the presence of something stirring deep within myself.

I let my breath out in snatches, a little at a time and, in order to divert myself, I bought a newspaper from a newsboy, opening it as I walked slowly along. As I did so, something jumped out at me. On the top left of the local news page was a photograph showing the smiling face of none other than Dr. Yamamoto. The headline, in large letters, pronounced:

> New Theory on Cure for Asthma
> Result of 30 Years' Research by Dr. Yamamoto
> U.S. Academic Circles Take Note

In my mind's eye I saw two long feelers growing out of the doctor's forehead. Then, one pair of short, trembling feelers, covered with fine hair, reached out towards me. For the first time, I felt the unmistakable harbinger of an asthma attack begin to crawl around inside me.

STRAW WEDDING CEREMONY

藁婚式

THE CRIMSON SEA STRETCHES out in the twilight beyond the hill. Such notions occasionally creep up on me, and, before I know it, suddenly the vision expands in my mind, but my mind cannot apprehend it. It swiftly seizes me, ensnaring me in abstraction; something in its colour goads me on, stinging.

Today, the westerly sky is aglow with the setting sun, and boiling leaden clouds cover the sky from the east. The wind, which has abruptly risen, passes over the ears of upland rice bending them towards the brightly lit sky—the cycle then repeating itself tempestuously again and again.

From near where the fields of upland rice peter out to the east and west, the land becomes a gentle slope, low hills on either side forming a damp basin in between. Neat modern dwellings with slate roofs are dotted here and there on the slope, though my house is in the hollow. The mountain ridge fuses with the twilight sky, concealing a shopping arcade around the suburban railway station.

Today too, the red surface of the sea extends beyond the hills. The colour gradually deepens, and before long the silhouette of a person appears unexpectedly near the water's edge, backlit against the ocean. The light forming the silhouette is dazzling, and I can't tell whether the figure's arms are raised or hanging down, or whether there is one person or in fact two. Before long, the silhouette vanishes suddenly and all that is left is the surface of the sea, which has turned deep red, rising and falling in a gentle undulation.

At length the vast expanse of water comes in and covers my eyes; I find myself in a room enclosed by dark grey walls.

I AM CROUCHING DOWN in that small, windowless room. Cradling my head in my arms, I bend over so that my chin almost touches my knees. Suddenly looking up, I see two men adopting the same posture, squatting down in two of the other corners of the room. In the middle of the room stands a woman. Throwing out her chest, she assumes an arrogant posture, and when I look closely I see that it is Mio. She comes to my room now and then.

I look away from her, and letting my gaze come to rest on the other two men I realise to my surprise they are virtually identical to me; it is as if we were triplets.

The same men assuming the same posture occupy three corners of this small room. Mio's lithe arm reaches out toward me. Her slender fingertips dig into my shoulder with a piercing strength and shake my body—which can offer no resistance from its squatting position—violently back and forth. Before long, I begin to cough, and the phlegm caught in my throat comes out of my mouth.

The coughs come incessantly, in rapid succession, and I have difficulty breathing. Thinking if there is blood mixed in with it I'm already done for, I wind some phlegm around my finger and draw it out of my mouth, peering at it, trying to find red streaks. Mio is tense too, and she appears to be staring at it with me, but there is no blood after all, and it ends with something like a shrivelled black globule of phlegm popping out. She turns away, a look of contempt on her face. My chest feels heavy as it did before. The pain becomes pretty severe until finally I wake up.

WHEN I OPEN MY eyes, I find Mio sitting by my side, and the myriad of water droplets that cling to her hair sparkle in the light of the electric lamp. Realising that my gaze has come to rest on her hair, she carefully wipes away the drops of water with a handkerchief and says, "I got caught in the rain, near that bridge over there. Look at this! I didn't think I would get so wet."

As I look out through the window, a pale, passing shower cuts diagonally through the dusky air, and a dull thrumming rises up all around—the legs of a steel-framed tower are visible in the near distance—the sound of thousands of volts of electricity discharging as raindrops fall onto the high-voltage cable running north to south far above the rooftops.

It had been raining the first time I met Mio too. With droplets of water sprinkled in her hair, she had looked obliquely up at me with sharp, flashing eyes and said simply and somewhat abruptly, "I like walking in the rain and getting wet. I never take an umbrella anywhere."

Speaking in a bright soprano voice, she had suddenly let out a short burst of laughter.

Today, sitting by my side, Mio wipes her moist skin with a handkerchief, rummages in her handbag, and takes out a sheet of writing paper that has been folded into quarters. Holding it out with her right hand, she says, "Now then, do you know what day it is today?"

A brilliant lustre seeps into her voice. I feel it is odd, and silently taking the piece of paper from her and opening it, I see that it contains her artless handwriting.

Candy wedding anniversary: 3 years
Straw wedding anniversary: 4 years
Wood wedding anniversary: 5 years
(Give a wooden item as a gift.)

"Say, that's right, isn't it? Four years have gone by already. I'll give you a present. Here, please take it."

Biting her lower lip slightly, she searches the bottom of her bag with a mischievous smile, takes out three wheat straws and places them on the tatami matting. Looking me quickly in the eye, her cheeks colour faintly.

"Well, I don't know. You talk about a 'straw wedding anniversary.' I wonder if it's . . ."

"It's true. It says so in the appendix to my diary," she says, with an earnest expression.

"The appendix to your diary?"

"If your lover's birthstone is April, that's a diamond, July: ruby, September: sapphire, November: topaz. A freesia means 'innocent friendship,' margaret: 'naïveté,' gardenia: 'happiness.'"

In my mind's eye, I see a woman copying down some of those words. Her expression, which is the image of Mio's, is filled with calm as she moistens the tip of her pencil.

The image is a little too much for me. Still wearing that expression on her face, she clings onto my back. Then we slither down together further into the distance. Repose to me is to be found in embracing a woman's body, all the while abandoning ourselves to the water that fills around us, sinking to the bottom in the endless faint light, the somewhat heavy feeling of the air that fills my lungs. During the four years that I have gradually sunk into her inner self, something has fallen away from her body. But she isn't aware of it. Behaving like an ordinary woman, she gradually reaches out toward that something she believes to be "happiness."

Picking up one of the wheat straws from the tatami matting, I hold its ends between two fingers and squash it flat. Then, as I wind it around my finger, it ruptures with the violent force of the air that finds its way out. The straws seem to be damp. One by one, I make the same sharp explosive noise with each of the three straws. While listening to the resonance I become irritated, finding myself not feeling entirely happy that an incident that occurred four years ago to the day continues to dwell in Mio's heart as is evidenced by her behaviour today and which manifests itself in her giving me a gift for our straw wedding anniversary.

Four years ago today.

That day too, a metallic whir spread out and filled the sky, and the sound of bombs exploding echoed in the distance. The day before that, I'd shown a chrome-plated key to Mio, and said, "Come with me tomorrow."

The muscles around her throat quivered sharply.

"I don't think you like me. Well, I don't like you either."

"Maybe that's why we feel miserable," I replied.

"Don't touch me. I make people unhappy."

Strangely, the self-demeaning tone of some of the phrases Mio used from time to time, together with her appearance, faintly tinged with despair, aroused my sexual desire for her. Her spindle-shaped body too—evident through her clothing— like some kind of aquatic animal, overpowered my senses.

That night my house was burned down in the air raids. As I sat on the foundation stones that had been swept by the flames, smoking a twisted cigarette, before I knew it she was standing in front of me. Her pupils dark and smiling only with her eyes, she said, "So, you didn't die."

Getting to my feet, I fished around in my pocket without saying anything. I showed her the chrome key I had in my hand, and asked, "Will you come with me?"

Mio lowered her eyes and murmured, "I'm tired."

As I began walking, she set off too and came along with me, muttering, "I'm tired, that's why."

As we picked our way along the railroad ties of the suburban train line, now suspended due to the war, the air raid siren sounded. Heading in the direction of a nearby river, we lay face down in a sloping meadow. With the azure sky reflected in the water of the wide river, the afternoon felt as though everything would suddenly disappear into thin air. I felt a little light-headed, and collapsed on top of Mio.

"You mustn't. You mustn't touch me."

Restraining my wrists from below, her thin, defiant voice inflamed my senses. Trapping her arms beneath my knees, I tore her blouse open wide with a sharp, almost metallic sound. Her radiant white skin protruded in two triangular mounds, on the tips of which, unexpectedly, were peach-blossom pink nipples. Tears flowed incessantly from the corners of her eyes—still open wide, as they were—streaking her colourful make-up.

Her eyes were rimmed with pale grey shadows and below her face—with its heavy, smudged lipstick—lay her body with its budding nipples pointing into the blue sky. Her white skin, which looked almost blue, reflected the glaring sunlight. Half unconsciously I reached out my arm, gathered her clothes, covered her exposed breasts and then sprawled on my back next to her. A single red wildflower wavered, almost covering our faces. I prodded the flower with my fingertip and it swayed languidly at the end of the stem.

"Fox peony, don't you think?"

"I wonder. Isn't it a torch lily?"

The flower—a kind of lily—was in full bloom. The tips of the radially aligned stamens were dusted with a crust of dark brown pollen. In the middle of the radial, the stigma of the pistil shone smoothly as if it were glass melted in a fire. Enticed by its colour, my finger was drawn towards the stigma. When the tip of my finger touched it very gently, it was moistened with mucilage and trailed a long thread. My back reverberating with the earth-shattering explosions in the distance, I felt my emotions boiling up within. I gazed at my wet fingertip and then unhurriedly drew near the dark brown pollen on the stigma.

Mio quite unexpectedly raised herself up and clung fast to my arm. She put my wet finger in her mouth and applied her teeth vigorously. Locked in that position, we collapsed amongst the grasses, and, like animals of human size, we entered a state of sexual intercourse all too easily. Looking into each other's eyes, we locked gazes and remained fixed in that position for quite some time. Then, Mio said, in a barely perceptible voice, "It's because I was tired. . . ." With a wry expression, she reached out her arm and covered my eyes with the palm of her hand. And yet she didn't draw away from me.

IT IS AS IF Mio has forgotten that four years have passed since that day.

In front of me, three bent wheat straws lie strewn on the tatami matting. Looking away for no reason, my eyes rest on a firefly on the glass door inside the room. It now and then emits light. I feel a sudden concentration of strength in my fingertips. Swiftly catching the insect, I sit down in front of Mio and show it to her.

"Let me give you a present too for our straw wedding anniversary. What do you think this is?"

"It's a firefly, isn't it?"

"No. It's like it, but it's a different insect," I say, continuing the explanation in a conclusive, grave tone, "Have you heard of a sea shell that crawls about if you immerse it in vinegar? This insect is truly a rare variety. . . .

"You take this insect, and . . . Let me explain. Then you place it on top of a sheet of white paper. The cold luminescence emitted from its body suddenly generates an unexpectedly high temperature and scorches the paper. As it crawls slowly along, the insect leaves behind a dark brown trail. But the heat doesn't only scorch the paper. It burns the insect's body, and before long the body itself disappears leaving behind on the white paper just a dark brown zigzag line where the insect had crawled along."

I place the insect on Mio's hand. Looking her in the eye, I say, "Go ahead. Try it."

Nodding once in agreement, she places it on the sheet of letter paper. The insect remains still for a while but soon spreads its wings and takes off. She follows its line of flight with her eyes, absent-mindedly muttering to herself, "Oh, it flew off."

With a keen creaking noise, the electric cables begin to sing in the distance. It looks like the wind has become a good deal stronger. Now and then we can hear the heavy beating of the wings of a moth, as if it is knocking on the window. In my mind's eye I see it suddenly sprinkling about yellow dust, like powder shed from torn leaves as they are plucked from a tree by the wind. The rain has almost become a storm. Then, the skirling of the wind dissipates, rooting itself deeply in my mind and distorting my mental image.

Now other voices can only reach me after passing through my warped outer shell.

Mio opens her mouth. The wind blows past with a hoarse whistle. Her words, which penetrate the threshold of my consciousness at that moment, are not real. It is not that I mind. It is just that my body suddenly feels exhausted.

The days and months over the last few years spent turning a woman, proud in every respect, into a model of obedience, weigh heavily on me, distorting the landscape of my mental picture.

I hear Mio speak. It is the sort of un-ladylike language she had used four years ago.

"Tell me. Are you ill?"

"I don't know."

"How pitiful! Ah, look here, I'll give you this."

Sitting relaxed, with her legs tucked sideways, she unfolds a banknote and dangles it in front of me with her fingertips. The banknote flutters in the wind blowing in through the gap in the window, and suddenly the smell of alcohol drifts out from between her lips.

"You idiot. Go home!"

I glare at her, my eyes flashing with anger, but she continues to behave as if nothing is the matter.

After a short time, while biting my lips so hard they turn white and blood seeps from them, I reach out unconsciously and take hold of the banknote. I sink my teeth into my arm, and blood oozes out from the blue vein. My palm, clutching the banknote, looks brown like a black man's hand.

"What are you playing at? Even if you bite it off there, it won't shed any red blood. Silly man. You don't know what you're doing."

"Shut up. You'd better go now."

"Aha! You've cheered up a bit. That's terrific."

"Go now. What the hell do you come here for anyway? Do you get a kick out of teasing me so much?"

"I don't have the time for that. It's because I love you, isn't it? But I prefer you the way you used to be. You were full of life, smart, and fun. Remember? I thought that was clever that time you said, 'Hey, I know that you have no belly button. If you want to prove you do, then show it to me.'"

"Damn!"

"Oh, what's this? Stroking where you bit yourself before, eh? Come on, you don't need to panic and stop doing it all of a sudden. You shouldn't have started it in the first place. Only tired, yellow blood would run out of a place like that. A rat wouldn't even be impressed."

"A rat?"

"A rat. That's what I said. There aren't even any rats in a room like this. They'd starve to death. You're beyond help. I'll give you these. Vienna sausages."

From the handbag by her side, Mio fishes out a skein of small, linked sausages and lays them, snake-like, on the tatami matting.

"What do you think? Are you ill?"

Once again, I hear her voice from beyond the thin veil.

"How about it? Wouldn't it be better to die? But then, if you're going to die, why not kill ten people you hate with a curse. That would be impressive. But I know you can't do it. You're useless now. You would just shrivel up and turn yellow."

"Kill someone with a curse? That's impossible."

"Of course it's possible! Even I've done it before. Men I hated, you understand. I'll make a straw doll. Or a paper doll, if you like. A stormy day like this is just perfect. I just stabbed the doll over and over with a hairpin. The first man was drunk and died falling into the Sumida River. The one after him, well, that was methyl. And the next, the door came off the train he was in and he fell out. And then . . ."

"And then, how many more before it's my turn?"

"It's not true! It's not true, I tell you! You're the first. That's why I've come here on a stormy day like this."

Then for a while there is a void . . .

Before long I hear Mio singing.

"Look, my dear Zenbei, you're ill, do you realise? You've got hepatitis. Zenbei's got hepatitis, Zenbei's got hepatitis. Oh, ho, ho, ho."

Needless to say, my name isn't Zenbei.

"Oh, I just remembered! Fat is bad for your liver. You shouldn't have sausages," she says.

As she speaks, the rope of small, linked sausages, lying on the tatami matting returns in an orderly fashion to her handbag. With my mouth agape, like an imbecile, I gaze at the scene before me. Just then, we begin to hear the proprietor of this apartment giving her young son a severe telling-off in one of the rooms downstairs.

Whenever Mio comes to visit me and stays a little time, this sturdy young widow in her thirties invariably begins to scold her young child.

Occasionally, the reedy voice that emanates from those lips drawn thinly back reaches maximum pitch before changing into a discordant squeal—the anguish of a woman in her thirties who can find no outlet for the frustration we cause her—and I would begin to hear the sound of the child sobbing its heart out. Fascinated, Mio narrows her eyes at that shrill voice, then, furiously knitting her brows together in an intense frown, she forces out a burst of staccato laughter, saying, "Oh, how stupid I am! You obviously have enough charm still to make a woman jealous. Can you believe it? Ha, ha, how funny."

The wind has died down considerably, though now and then raindrops spatter against the windows.

Then it seems some languid music is playing nearby. Usually when Mio hears the reproving voice of the widow downstairs, her eyes reveal her fear, but not this time. Besides, this thirty-something woman stopped dressing her child down ten days or so ago.

Gradually I am pulled back into the here and now, and the melancholy sound filling the area round about begins to take on a definite form. It sounds like a chanson being played on the gramophone downstairs.

Spring flowers have yet to open
Flowers of love will no longer bloom
Gloomy, gloomy, gloomy Sunday. . . .

"Say, what's the matter?"

Mio's frightened eyes grow bigger. I lean my back against the wall, and she shakes my knees.

"I thought the wind was blowing a gale before."

"It was. But it's calmed down a lot now."

Maybe I'd dozed off. I feel a heavy sense of lethargy all over. The music rising up from downstairs has been playing that monotonous melody for some time now. Straining my ears and trying to catch the lyrics, I realise they are in French. The heavy, low female voice brimming with lingering deep sorrow seems to be singing the lyrics of the song that passed through my mind earlier.

The reason why the woman downstairs has stopped scolding her young son, it is safe to say, can be found in the melody of that song. But it doesn't follow that she is playing that record because she is in a melancholic frame of mind.

During the seven or so years since she has become a widow, she raised her child, making ends meet, without wearing any makeup at all. And, because she has remained chaste, her waist has grown as thick as her hips. Or perhaps because she is that shape to begin with, there is no particular hint of romance about her; it isn't really clear which is the case.

She is a paragon of virtue in everything she does and says. She readily criticises a relationship like the one I have with Mio, her persecution of us taking a wide variety of forms.

When Mio was visiting me, the woman downstairs would rattle the house by opening and closing the sliding paper screens and then, before long, she would continue to reprimand her young child in her shrill voice.

To be fair she is under a lot of pressure; social conditions no longer permit a single woman to live on the proceeds of a modest side job.

Finally, about two weeks ago, she said to me, "From now on I won't be home in the evenings. So, if you go out, make sure you lock up, you understand? I can't put food on the table, so I've decided to become a dancer."

I feel embarrassed relating such a trite and dull story. So, let me bring it to an end as quickly as possible.

One evening about a week later, she brought a customer home and there began a bout of drinking. Excited by these unusual and lively goings-on, the shrill voice of the high-spirited child continued deep into the night, mixed with the echoes of the boisterous party. Before long, the child's voice died away, and all fell abruptly quiet.

For me, this is a truly disappointing and, in a sense, pitiful story. But, I was in for a shock if I thought the music downstairs reflected my landlady's heartfelt sorrow. A sad tale indeed—there is something a little lacking in her heart which leads me to interpret her situation in that way.

There are those who blame me for stealing something from them. But the truth is they take things from me; yet I am so embarrassed by their behaviour I pretend not to notice. I have experienced something similar with this woman. She doesn't see my hidden embarrassment. But do not be deceived. Even if women in pink rayon tops and baggy trousers with bibs advertising the name of a dance hall, M—D, sewn on their chests, attract attention by playing baseball in an open area downtown, there is no ulterior motive to their behaviour.

"Hey! Come on! Oh my!"

Putting her arm around my neck, Mio draws close to my ear and whispers softly, "Say . . ."

She's pregnant, on a windy day like this. Those words suddenly come into my mind, and soon my eyes shine coldly. The thought of someone being born into this world with my blood coursing through its veins—I would pity the child.

I mentally calculate the amount of money I would need to raise the child. Suddenly I hear Mio say something I am not expecting.

"Say, what I just said, it was a lie. It was a lie, I tell you."

I turn my intense gaze on her and look her squarely in the eye. She bats her eyelids two or three times and then brushes her eyelashes down all at once. Only my earnest mood is left helplessly behind.

I enquire, in a somewhat harsh tone, "Why did you tell me such a lie?"

"Because, however much I try talking to you, you don't answer me at all. You're in a world of your own. So, I thought I would shock you. It's not such a bad thing to be shocked."

"You may be right. It wasn't so bad, actually," I murmur, softly.

Then, suddenly standing up, I take hold of her shoulders, shake her vigorously, and say, "Why are you looking so gloomy? Today's our straw wedding anniversary; that's cause for a big celebration, isn't it?"

"Yes. But, what shall we do?"

"You silly. Let's go downstairs and dance. It's her profession, you know. It's what she does for a living. She's bound to let us have a good time."

Taking Mio by the hand, I pull her to her feet and we start down the stairs. Under my arm, I can feel her waist as thick as the landlady's hips.

Spring flowers have yet to open
Flowers of love will no longer bloom
But we will go far
Holding a woman and dancing together
Those hips like a barrel
I shall hold them and swing to the rhythm of the song
Gloomy, gloomy, gloomy Sunday. . . .

Singing nonsensical lyrics to myself, I go down the stairs with deliberately heavy footsteps. A hesitant footfall comes clip-clopping down behind me.

Midnight Stroll

深夜の散歩

I couldn't help being afraid of my landlady in Shinjuku.

Though I was a university student, there was a curfew at my lodgings, ten o'clock in the evening at that.

After I'd returned late two nights in a row from drinking with friends, my landlady proclaimed, "Students should be studying. From now on, I'll be locking the door at ten o' clock. Please make sure you are back by then."

She was a large-boned woman, a prim and proper widow who didn't believe in wearing makeup. Since losing her husband to illness during the upheaval following the war, she had raised her school-age son, making ends meet by taking in sewing, knitting and the like. Her behaviour was impeccable, and she never did anything that would cause people to talk about her behind her back.

She was morally upright in everything she did and said, and announcing a ten o'clock curfew was yet another manifestation.

I was quite unable to quarrel with her. Her high moral stance was simple and clear, without any hint of human kindness. To make matters worse, she obstinately defended her point of view, without attempting to advance her argument. That being the case, I was unable to get a hold of anything to argue about. We were playing by different rules, so a quarrel never materialised. But worse still, she would stand there, fists on hips, stout legs firmly braced and sticking out from a skirt resembling a rice sack. Her watchful eyes would scowl at me from out of a florid, un-made-up face, and then she would shower me with moralising vitriol. Faced with this onslaught, I would soon lose the will to argue back.

Her appearance was in keeping with her tirade, and I felt she was flatly incapable of understanding my position.

I COULDN'T HELP BEING afraid of my landlady, and it was pointless arguing with her. But then neither did I obey the curfew; violating it was my way of protesting.

Returning home around midnight I would knock on the front door. With the lights in the house off, it would be pitch black. I would knock persistently until, at length, a pale shadow would fall across the glass pane and the door would open inwards with a harsh creak.

"Don't you realise it's the middle of the night? The curfew was hours ago!"

"If you wouldn't mind putting an end to the curfew, then I'd make sure I was home much earlier."

"What nonsense! If you're able to return earlier, then you should do so, shouldn't you?"

I fell silent. In response, she said, in a spiteful tone, "I regret giving lodgings to someone like you. I really do regret it."

"Well, I regret lodging in a house like this too."

"If that's how you feel, then why don't you leave?"

"No, I don't think I will."

When I considered the trouble I would have to put myself to in order to move out, I didn't feel I could be bothered. I had become obstinate as well.

The next day too I returned around midnight and rapped on the door. I knocked several times, but the door remained shut.

Climbing up the fence, I walked across the roof and made my way over to the window of my room on the second floor. It was a small house, with two rooms on the ground floor and one upstairs, and I was the only lodger. From the window I was able to gain access to my room without mishap. From then on, I always entered my room through the window whenever I returned after the curfew. The landlady never locked the window on the inside, my means of entering the house late tacitly accepted.

I always returned in the exact same sequence—fence, roof, and then window; it was as good as if the curfew had ceased to exist. As a consequence, I lost my enthusiasm for loitering around outside until late and could always be found in my second-floor room at ten o'clock each night.

MY RELATIONS WITH MY landlady, though, became more and more stormy.

The situation was compounded by a minor incident.

I'd got into the habit of lying in bed and reading until late into the night and then getting off to sleep after I'd been to the toilet. Whenever I came down from the second floor, the cheaply constructed, narrow stairway made a creaking sound. Since I was well-built, the stairs gave out an even higher pitched squeal than usual, and the creaking sound would reverberate shrilly throughout the hushed house.

When I had knocked on the door in the middle of the night, I had done so determinedly, and I didn't hesitate to wake the occupants of this dark, quiet dwelling.

But this was different, and I was afraid of disturbing the sleep of those downstairs, who would be very sensitive to the creaking sound. And so, watching my step, I would come down the stairs as quietly and slowly as possible. I became rather tired of this routine after a while.

One evening, when I reached the bottom of the stairs, a faint shadow waited in front of the lavatory. Sure enough, it was the landlady.

"Please, go ahead," I said.

To which she replied, "No, it's alright. Please, Mr. Yamamura [that's my name], you go first."

"No. No. Please, you first."

"No, I insist."

Confronted by my landlady's stout frame as she stood in front of the lavatory entrance, I was unable to move an inch. Perhaps she realised this, for she moved aside.

Making my way past her, I went into the toilet and was assailed by a strange feeling. As I slipped past her, a feminine odour mingled with the fragrance of perfume came suddenly to me.

Though I closed the lavatory door, I could sense that she was still standing in front of it. Whenever someone's waiting for me to finish my business, I become self-conscious and can't urinate properly.

The more I tried to hurry, the worse it was. Taking my time didn't seem reasonable either, so, giving it up, I came out. Looking as though I'd finished what I'd gone in there to do, I said, "Excuse me for going first."

"Not at all."

A strangely feminine voice came from the faint shadow standing outside the door—so much so that, for a moment, I suspected my ears were playing me false and it was someone else standing there. My landlady was waiting patiently as before, and I made my way past her. Once again, the fragrance of perfume tickled the back of my nose.

I went back to my room on the second floor and, after a short while, the urge to urinate intensified, but I couldn't bring myself to go down those creaking stairs again. Besides, I was afraid of going down there right now. That feminine odour, intermingled with the fragrance of perfume, and the unusually gentle timbre of her voice brought something vividly to mind. Then, not at all sure of the reason why, I felt afraid. It was then that something occurred to me as a means of last resort: I would open my window and urinate on the roofing tiles. There was no other way to alleviate the situation.

I realised that this method was very convenient. Depending on the angle the fluid struck the roofing tiles, I could finish my business hardly making any noise.

Ah, yes, this is definitely the solution to my problem! I murmured to myself.

Above all else, using this method saved the bother of having to go downstairs. Secondly, I no longer had to worry about the creaking stairs. And thirdly, my landlady would be freed from having her sleep disturbed in the middle of the night. It was a good way of killing three birds with one stone.

I continued with this method for seven days. Then, on the morning of the eighth day, I was woken from my slumber by a shrill, piercing scream.

"Mr. Yamamura! Please get up!"

The voice came from the direction of the garden. It repeated itself, impatiently, several times, and the tone suggested it wasn't a trifling matter. Getting up, I put my head out the window. As I did so, I was confronted by my landlady who was standing in the garden glaring in my direction with a fierce expression on her face.

"Would you please come down here for a moment and look at this."

"What's the matter?"

"Never mind *what's the matter.* There's moss growing on the ground below the drainpipe. I'm sure the drainpipe is starting to rot as well."

I wasn't inclined to explain to her my idea of killing three birds with one stone. I was sure she wouldn't appreciate my delicate consideration. Moreover, while I didn't realise it at the time, apparently she wasn't annoyed with me merely because of my ill manners and the drainpipe which had begun to rot. But this occurred to me only later.

MY GIRLFRIEND CAME TO visit me in my room at the lodgings. From that day forward, my relationship with my landlady became stormier still. It appeared that the visit of a young woman to a bachelor's room had affronted her moral values.

Then it happened that she frequently opened and closed the doors with a harsh bang. It felt as if the house were filled with finely broken glass which pierced my skin.

On one particular occasion, after she had carried on like this for several days, she confronted me suddenly and announced, "I have decided that from tomorrow I shall work in a cabaret. You see, it's got to the stage where I really can't make a living as things stand."

Bewildered, I fell silent for a while; I couldn't readily understand the connection between my landlady and a cabaret girl.

For the first time I thought about her age. When I considered it, even if she were twelve years older than I she would still only be about thirty five.

In my mind I tried to substitute that rice sack of a skirt for a gaudy, colourful one. I attempted to apply heavy makeup to that florid face, normally devoid of cosmetics. But try as I might, all that came to mind was a vague and, if anything, grotesque image. Be that as it may, she was still attractive enough; in fact, she was a woman in her prime.

Suddenly I recalled that recent night when I had slipped past her in front of the lavatory. I remembered vividly the feminine odour, mingled with the fragrance of perfume. Why on earth had she applied perfume that particular evening, though she seldom ever did?

As I began to ponder that question, her voice rang out.

"And so you see, if I do that I won't be able to look after you, Mr. Yamamura, the way I have done. I need you to find other lodgings as quickly as possible. I have even arranged for a relative to look after my son for a while."

She says she's looked after me, but I wonder how exactly. I don't take my meals in this house. I eat in the school cafeteria, or at restaurants in town. But now she's said it, I'll have to think about looking somewhere else.

"Oh really? In that case, I'll try and sort something out," I replied, continuing to stare at her. For the life of me, I couldn't imagine how she would be with customers at the cabaret.

A look of puzzlement must have stayed on my face, because she said, in a defensive tone of voice, "My younger sister works in a cabaret. She's been begging me to come."

Now she mentioned it, from time to time just recently I had noticed a heavily made-up woman who gave off an intensely feminine odour, and I realised it was her younger sister.

WHEN I SET OFF for school shortly before noon on the day she began working at the cabaret, she was just the way she'd always been.

That night, a friend invited me out for a drink. Unusually for me, I arrived back at the lodgings well past the curfew of 10 o'clock. As was my custom, I approached the small, two-storey house intent on climbing the fence and entering my room via the roof.

As I did so, I noticed that the lights in the house, until now always dark, were burning brightly.

I stopped nearby. A winsome voice interwoven with an inebriated man's tones carried outside the house. I was startled, and it distressed me to recall this was my landlady's first day at the cabaret.

I went round to the garden. Through the glass door facing the garden I could make out two couples dancing, though it would be more accurate to describe it as two drunken couples locked together in boisterous merrymaking. It seemed likely the men were cabaret customers and the other woman was my landlady's younger sister.

The lively voices sounded intermittently, and the image in the glass door swayed in an exaggerated way.

"This is a little fast off the mark for your first day, isn't it?" I muttered to myself.

I recalled my landlady's high-minded way of talking and her virtuous expression. Those moralising words of hers had been utterly lacking in feeling. Still, her words must have concealed some warmth welling up somewhere inside her.

Feeling wretched, I gazed at the scene reflected in the glass door. I didn't want her to know I was there. Before long, the spree inside the house would probably die down, the bright lights would dim and a different night would begin. No doubt a different kind of merrymaking would then commence.

I didn't particularly wish to stick around in order to witness the transition. The two men in the house wouldn't have recognised the landlady as the woman she had been until this morning; they were no doubt delighted with their unexpected good fortune in this romantic adventure.

I didn't feel curious enough to keep listening to what was going on in the house. I couldn't even bring myself to ridicule the change in my landlady who, until only a few hours before, had been the very picture of morality.

I was seized only by a violent feeling of pity and rawness that put a damper on what was occurring. I no longer wanted to see my landlady, or be seen by her; I wanted to hide from it all. Walking on tiptoe, I stole quietly away.

I walked fifteen minutes from my lodgings, emerging at a suburban railway station. The lights were still on in the station precincts.

It was past 1:00 a.m., but the last southbound train was still waiting there. I recalled there was a station by a river five stops away and, boarding the last train, I decided to go there.

I didn't think it a bad idea to spend the night by the river either.

Getting off at my destination, I walked in the direction of the river. The air on this summer's evening was sultry.

Along the way I came across a dense wood. The air became unexpectedly cool, and the sound of my footfalls on the ground echoed loudly.

Just then, a large, black shadow of a man appeared from behind the thick trunk of a tree. He seemed to be standing still and looking in my direction. I gathered myself. I sensed he was breathing quietly as he watched me.

The man took two or three steps toward me. I could hardly hear his footsteps.

"Hey, anything the matter? What are you doing?"

It was the voice of a man, deep and with a hard edge to it, but it wasn't menacing at all.

"I'm taking a walk," I replied.

"A walk? What, in the middle of the night?"

"I can't go back to my lodgings."

"How come?"

I made no reply.

"You afraid of your mother?"

"I'm afraid of my landlady," I replied, disarmed by what he'd said.

"Ha-ha-ha!" Laughing loudly, he replied, "Is that right? In that case, let's take a stroll together." Taking the lead, he set off walking and moved out of the wood.

As we came out of the trees, I could see by the light of the moon that he wore a round-neck shirt and had a towel wrapped around his neck. He was a large, powerfully built man, shoulders and back rippling with bulging muscles.

Around his legs he had on something resembling close-fitting 'patchi' silk drawers, and on his feet he wore rubber-soled work tabi—the reason why I hadn't been able to hear his footsteps earlier. He had a livery coat over one arm, and he looked like a labourer.

The large man stared at me and said, "Well, I was afraid, seeing such a big guy come into the woods, I can tell you."

"It was me that was afraid! But why are you in the woods in the dead of night?"

"I drank too much and it got late. I'm afraid of my wife, so I can't go home," he said. "Even so, I went close, but like I said, I was scared and couldn't bring myself to go inside. I crawled into the hen coop in the garden and tried sleeping there. But it was no good; I was nearly bitten to death by mosquitoes and couldn't lie still for very long at all."

"Is that right? Is your wife such a scary person?"

"She certainly is. You just said you were afraid of your land-lady and couldn't go home, right? Well, my wife is a lot scarier!"

He came to a halt and gazed at me.

"I thought I'd find somewhere cool and try and get some sleep, but the wood is full of stinging bugs. I figured I'd have to wander around and kill time until morning. You arrived just at the right time. Do you fancy a stroll? I'll show you around," said the man, and began to walk.

Thinking it would be a useful way of idling away time 'til dawn, I followed. With a gait suggesting he was well acquainted with this neighbourhood, he weaved his way along the narrow roads that wound their way between the houses. After turning several corners, the view suddenly opened up. The houses disappeared and fields stretched out around us. The man walked quickly along the narrow paths that ran between the fields. His feet, with their rubber-soled *tabi*, barely made a sound. His powerful back—wrapped in the white round-neck shirt—loomed in front of me.

He made his way silently through the fields.

I became uneasy. The fields began to peter out, and the black shadow of a new coppice drew near.

Just as I thought of asking where he planned on going he stopped and turned around.

"Have you got a little money?"

I was startled. I knew I had a five hundred yen note in my trouser pocket. "I think I have about five hundred yen."

"Is it alright to use that?"

"Sure."

"Well then, let me take you to a Torys bar. I'm completely broke."

He set off walking again. Coming out of the coppice, there was a small town. He'd walked through the fields simply as a shortcut.

It was gone 1:00 a.m., but the Torys bar was still open. There was just a lone, middle-aged man in one of the booths, and in one corner, a young couple sat with their arms around one another's shoulders, talking in whispers.

Downing a whisky in one gulp, the man turned his head in the direction of the couple and said, "That's nice, huh?"

After draining another whisky, he yelled, "It's alright for some. I'm really envious."

Then, turning to face me, he enquired, "You've a fine build. What do you do for a living?"

"I'm a student."

"A student, you say? You're wasted being a student."

"Well then, what should I be?"

"A labourer."

He finished off yet another drink, then turned his head toward the couple in the dark corner, and said, this time looking to me for agreement, "It's alright for some. Don't you think?"

I didn't say anything. Before long the couple stood up and, as they left the bar, the proprietor said, "It's already well past closing time, I'm afraid. I'll have to ask you to start making your way home."

We went out again onto the nighttime road. Planting his feet firmly, the man surveyed his surroundings.

"This area used to be the red-light district. After it went downhill, they switched to bars and hotels. It seems there was a loophole in the law. How about it, shall we wander around and take a look?"

We started to walk. What looked like small eateries lined both sides of the narrow road. The buildings were side-on to the road, their windows open as it was a humid summer's night.

Whenever we happened across an open window we would take a peek. Inside one, a man and woman lay asleep next to one another, exhausted. The woman snuggled close to the man's chest. His cotton kimono was open wide at the chest, and the hem of the woman's robe was in disarray.

"Oh, they're sleeping, tired out after a bout in bed," said the man, again looking to me for agreement. "Aren't you jealous?"

I said nothing. On this particular night, even seeing a man and woman nestled close to one another didn't arouse within me the slightest feeling of envy.

Ever since I'd left my lodgings, where the lights had been burning brightly, I'd felt nothing but gloom heavy on my heart.

"Aren't you envious?" pressed the man, again.

"Well, . . ." I replied, noncommittally.

"You're a student, you said. Don't give yourself airs!"

Flustered, I replied, "I'm not putting on airs. I don't know why, but I feel strange tonight."

Just then, we came across a window on the left with a light on. Inside, a woman sat alone in front of a small, low dining table, eating. A fleshy individual, she sat with her legs folded to one side, wearing a petticoat and bolting down a bowl of rice and tea. Slices of pickled radish were piled up on one side of the plate.

"Hey, they look tasty," said the man, sticking his head through the window.

"They certainly are good."

"Could you spare a slice of that pickled radish?"

She picked a slice of radish from the plate with her fingers and popped it in the man's mouth.

With an energetic chewing noise, he spat out his words unreservedly, "How about coming out with us tonight?"

"So long as you have some money. It won't do to be stingy, you know," she replied, relaxing still more. The fleshy insides of her thighs came quickly into view.

In that instant, I was seized by the desire to attack her, to torment her until her very flesh and bones creaked. Was that sexual desire? Or perhaps it was a desire to exact revenge for the nebulous fear I felt toward this thing called 'woman.' Either way, the impulse soon faded, replaced by the oppressive realisation I couldn't return home for another four hours.

I RECKONED IT WOULD be alright to return to my lodgings after 8:00 a.m.

I figured the guests were probably office workers and they would have left by then. I killed time sitting on a bench at the station, arriving at my lodgings at 8 a.m. It seemed the guests had gone home, for the front door was unlocked.

My skin was sticky with sweat and dew from walking around all night. Entering the house I headed straight for the washroom. Though I called it the washroom, it was really the kitchen sink, and it was there that I suddenly came face to face with my landlady. Her eyes were bloodshot with fatigue and alcohol, and her face swollen.

When she saw me she looked embarrassed and lowered her eyes.

Then, in a despairing tone, she said, "Oh, are you back now? Everything's at sixes and sevens, isn't it?"

I didn't say anything. I couldn't see her face directly. I hadn't stayed out all night through any sense of carefree abandon, nor had she. All I thought was that perhaps even my landlady, whose warmth and feeling were seeping out in front of my very eyes, would have a more meaningful life opening up before her.

Flowers

花束

Hooking his finger into the dial of the telephone, he hesitated for a moment; he continued to hesitate and then dialled the number.

The telephone's ringing began to sound softly in the receiver. He felt like hanging up there and then.

Having not the slightest idea what the surroundings were like around the ringing telephone made him feel ill at ease. His anxiety was sure to diminish somewhat if he knew, for example, that the telephone was on top of the chest of drawers in the living room and that Sugiko would get up and answer it if it rang. Since it was a Thursday afternoon, her husband ought to have been out at work.

He knew only what the outside of her house looked like. Once, several years ago, he'd stealthily walked around that neighbourhood and taken a look. It was a solid, Western-style building, utterly inaccessible to the likes of him.

He'd intended walking around in a casual manner, but he suddenly realised he was creeping about on tiptoe. His behaviour was pitiful, and he never went near Sugiko's house again. Whilst the external appearance remained vividly in his mind, even now he had no idea about the inside of the house; he didn't even know which room the telephone was in.

It didn't seem as though anyone was going to answer. The wait was causing him distress, and he started to ring off. It was the first chance he'd had of telephoning Sugiko in six years. He decided to hang up and call again at a different time, but he felt down when he thought about having to dial afresh, and he knew he couldn't let this opportunity slip by.

Just then someone at the other end lifted the receiver.

"Hello?"

He heard a young woman's voice, but it didn't sound like Sugiko.

"Is that Ms. Sonoda's house?"

Whenever he mentioned that family name he fell into a gloomy, irritable mood. He felt uncomfortable saying the surname of the man she'd married. He wondered whether it was the maid's voice, in which case Sugiko's discipline in the house was clearly lacking. Had she trained the maid to answer the phone and say something like, "This is the Sonoda residence," then he wouldn't have had to refer to that family name.

"Is that Ms. Sonoda's house?"

"Yes."

"Is Sugiko there? My name is Uokawa."

"Just a moment please."

There was a brief interval, and then he heard her voice.

"Mr. Uokawa, it's been quite a while, hasn't it? How many years is it? Well now, what can I do for you, I wonder."

It was a lifeless, melancholy voice.

"You ought to know what I want whenever I telephone. Do you mean it's alright to call you about something else?"

Silence . . .

"You asked how long it's been. It's six years already. The last time was the seventh anniversary of Kizaki's death and this will be the thirteenth."

His tone wasn't demanding but sounded more like a grumbling complaint.

"That's right. It was, wasn't it?" replied Sugiko, in the same tone as before.

"The anniversary is next Tuesday. Shall I drop by your house then and pick you up?"

Up until six years ago they would arrange to meet at a National Railways station close by Kizaki's house. During that time, Uokawa had been promoted to section chief.

But even he himself had heard rumours within the company that his trustworthiness was his only redeeming feature and that he would advance no further than department head at best.

Sugiko thought for a moment, "Yes, I'd like that. But, I wonder if you know where I live."

As a result of the trouble he'd gone to several years ago to search out her house, a map of the neighbourhood was clearly engraved on his memory. And yet, what he actually said was, "Well then, can you give me some rough directions?"

WHEN HE WENT TO the house on that Tuesday and rang the bell, Sugiko came to the entrance right away, having dressed to go out. The door to the house closed behind her.

The car was a hire vehicle he'd requested from work. They drove along without saying anything for a while, but, before long, Sugiko broke the silence.

"Mr. Uokawa, did you remarry?"

"No, I'm still single."

Kizaki had met his untimely death in a traffic accident, and then, just after the third anniversary of his death, Sugiko had got married. Shortly afterwards, Uokawa was married too, though a year later he lost his wife.

"Do you have children, Sugiko?"

"No."

"You must be lonely then. I'm surprised you don't have any kids."

"That's all very well, but it's impossible. Didn't you know?"

"Uh?"

"Sonoda died, you see."

"What?" Aware that his voice had come across as an exclamation of joy, he quickly adopted a grave tone. "I had no idea. Was it a traffic accident as well?"

"It was a heart attack."

"Is that right? When did it happen?"

"It was the year after the seventh anniversary of Kizaki's death, so that would be . . . But, Mr. Uokawa, you're being a little nosy, aren't you?"

"Eh?"

"I didn't think I needed to go to the thirteenth anniversary. A dead person is a dead person. That's all there is to it. Those left behind have their own lives to lead," said Sugiko firmly. "After I was married, I didn't feel like going to Kizaki's anniversary gathering any longer. But, you wouldn't have it, and asked me to go anyway."

They fell silent for a while. Then he said, indecisively, "But, today will be the last time. . . ."

"Yes, I agree. Today's the last time."

"Oh, driver, would you stop for a moment in front of that florist over there?"

He got out of the car and went into the florist's shop then returned carrying a bouquet of flowers made up entirely of white chrysanthemums.

"Why don't you take the flowers? It's more becoming that way."

"White chrysanthemums, eh? It was always just white chrysanthemums," said Sugiko, somewhat quietly, looking down at the bouquet on her lap.

At the time of the first anniversary, he'd tried to have the florist put together a bouquet of various flowers, but Sugiko had said they were only to be white chrysanthemums.

At that time, Sugiko had wept openly in front of the Kizaki family's Buddhist altar. During the funeral, her eyelids were so swollen from crying she could hardly open her eyes. She was to have married Kizaki. He was twenty seven at the time of his death, and she was five years his junior.

Uokawa had waited in tense expectation, but in the end she'd married another man, and the only time he was able to see her after that was once a year on the anniversary of Kizaki's death.

The car reached the vicinity of Kizaki's house but then lost its way. Finally locating the garden nursery that served as a landmark, he and Sugiko got out of the car. He walked on ahead while she held the flowers. The building next door but one to the garden nursery store should have been the house they were looking for, but it was now a vacant lot, and the ancient-looking two-storey dwelling he remembered was no longer there.

Signs of recent site preparation remained on the vacant lot, and to the rear stood a small, two-storey building.

"That two-storey place—I wonder if it was there before," he said to Sugiko.

"Let me think. "

"Wait here. I'll just try asking at that house."

She remained on the road holding the flowers while he walked up to the house.

Night had fallen as they were on their way there. He drew near the house, but he couldn't tell whether it was newly built, and not simply because it was dark.

It even resembled the shape of Kizaki's house. He looked for the nameplate on the post at the entrance but couldn't find one.

The window on the second floor was dark, and there was only one window downstairs reflecting any light. The door to the entrance wasn't locked. Standing on the concrete floor, he called out.

He called two or three times, each time raising his voice a little higher, but there was no reply. Stepping outside, he walked up to the window with the light. A lattice had been fitted to the window, and he tried calling through the glass.

"Wait a minute," came the voice of a young girl.

At that moment he heard the sound of water. He guessed the bathroom must be on the other side of the window. Once again, he stood on the concrete floor of the entrance and waited.

After a little while a woman appeared, and he recognised her as Kizaki's mother. She had a healthy glow about her, and he noticed steam rising faintly from her skin – as if she'd just emerged from the bath. He realised then that it had been her voice he'd heard, and not that of a young girl.

Kizaki's mother looked young, even younger than when he'd met her six years before. Kizaki's father was his real father, but she was his stepmother. Since there was only about ten years' difference between her and Kizaki, she would have been thirty-seven or eight when he died. But, being modest and gentle, she played the part of his mother to perfection.

In the eyes of Uokawa, several years out of university, that heartbroken figure looked to him like a mother devastated by the death of her own son, and that, he reflected, is how it must have seemed to everyone.

Every year on the anniversary of his death, she welcomed Sugiko and Uokawa, who would visit bringing flowers, with a grateful attitude and told them about her memories of her son.

Kizaki's stepmother must have been about fifty now, though she didn't look her age at all. Her skin, fresh from bathing, was peach-blossom pink and radiated a sense of beauty.

Looking at him standing there forlornly, she said, "Dear me! Mr. Uokawa, it really has been a long time," and an expression flashed across her face which suggested she was trying to recall something.

When her expression settled itself, she knelt down with her knees together on the step to the entrance hall. But it wasn't an attitude of welcome; rather, it looked as though she was barring his way.

"I thought today was the thirteenth anniversary of Kizaki's death, and so . . ."

He realised his tone sounded defensive.

"Yes, that's right. I just came back this evening from a visit to the grave with relatives. I had no idea that you would come, Mr. Uokawa."

It didn't appear that anyone else was in the house. Leastways, it didn't seem as though there would be many people there.

Maybe it would be better to just place some joss sticks in front of the family's Buddhist altar, and then go right back home, thought Uokawa.

As if reading his thoughts, she said, having arranged her knees more formally, "We have taken his mortuary tablet back to his hometown, and so I can't even ask you to offer up incense sticks. But really, Mr. Uokawa, thank you very much for coming."

An interminable smile remained on her face. It looked taut and fixed in place.

"Well, then, I was going to ask about Kizaki's father. . . ."

"Oh dear, perhaps I didn't notify you. He passed away the year before last."

"Did he really? Oh, I see. . . ."

Silence descended. Her posture, in sitting upright on the step to the entrance, was an unequivocal rejection of his presence, and he was unable to keep the conversation going.

"I see, . . ." he said, once more. "Well, then, I suppose I'll be going."

A faint smile appeared again on her face, and she looked relieved.

"I'm really sorry I can't ask you to come in."

He didn't feel like telling her he'd come with Sugiko. That would have made her all the more tense, and it would have caused Sugiko unnecessary discomfort too.

He returned to where Sugiko was standing, waiting on the road. The bunch of chrysanthemums she held in her arms rose up, dimly white.

Handing the bouquet to him, like a heavy piece of luggage, she said, "You were gone quite a while, weren't you?"

Silence . . .

"Did you find out where Kizaki's house is?"

"We won't be needing these flowers any more. Here, why don't you take them home with you."

Having briefly taken the bunch of flowers, he presented them to her, as though making an offering.

"I don't want them," she said, pressing them back into his arms.

WHEN THEY RETURNED TO the car, Sugiko asked again, "Did you figure out which was his house?"

"It was the one we saw just now."

She looked at him with a questioning gaze.

He briefly explained what had happened in the entrance to the house and told her about Kizaki's stepmother's suspicious behaviour.

"Is that right?"

Her tone sounded as though she was saying, "See, I told you as much."

"A dead person is a dead person. Those left behind have their own lives to lead."

It was as if Sugiko was trying to convince herself that this was true.

"As I said, Mr. Uokawa, you were too nosy."

Her voice had a reproachful ring to it.

"Maybe you're right."

He lowered his eyes. The large bouquet that Sugiko had insisted on handing back to him earlier lay on his lap.

"I don't think it's a bad thing to be nosy, but, you're nosy in things that don't concern you. I still remember the story of you catching that robber when you were a student, you know."

Silence . . .

"Even if there is a fourteenth anniversary gathering, I won't be going to Kizaki's house again."

"Me neither. Today will be the last time."

The silence continued as the car drove along.

"Oh, please stop over there."

The street corner where the car pulled over was quite a distance from Sugiko's house.

"I'm just going to drop by somewhere on my way home."

"Oh, really?"

"Goodbye, Mr. Uokawa."

The car moved off. Leaning back against the seat, he closed his eyes.

Sugiko had mentioned the story about the robber, and the recollection came back to him together with a disagreeable overtone.

It was far from a tale of heroic exploits and wasn't, in fact, worthy of being referred to as a robbery at all. At the time, he'd been riding on a packed train. The train stopped, and a young man reached up for a package on the luggage rack, tucked it under his arm and got off at the station.

He happened to know that the package belonged to another man, and, quick as a thought, he followed the young man outside. Elbowing his way through the crowd on the platform, he pursued the man. He hunched over, and moved stealthily, as though he were hunting his prey, and he felt a hot passion welling up within him.

Prepared to pursue the man doggedly to the ends of the earth, as the man passed in front of a police box, he reported the matter to the police officer and had him arrested. Afterwards, he had explained the circumstances to Kizaki and Sugiko.

He'd begun to talk with a sense of pride, but by the time he'd finished his account, he was feeling dismal. Perhaps the expressions of Kizaki and Sugiko as they listened to his story were reflected in his mind. Recalling the passionate feeling he'd experienced while chasing the man made him feel miserable that he'd spent so much youthful zeal on something like that.

The passion he felt for Sugiko had no outlet. He recalled the posture he'd adopted while pursuing the man, and the word *sneak* came to mind. It meant to crawl about on the ground. Afterwards, he felt as though he'd left behind a glutinous, slug-like trail. Now, over a decade later, he was forced to endure that feeling again.

Moving the bouquet from his lap, he set it down where Sugiko had been sitting. For a moment he thought about going for a drink but then gave up on the idea. He wasn't a drinker. He felt a strong urge to go home right away and lie down.

The car stopped in front of his house. Prompted by the driver, he retrieved the bouquet, and, taking the key out of his pocket, he opened the front door.

His maid had got married and quit her job, and he hadn't gotten around to finding a replacement.

He gazed for a while at the bouquet he'd tossed onto the desk.

"What a cold bunch of flowers," he murmured. The flowers had an excessive number of leaves, stiff right to the tips of their veins, which seemed to soar into the air.

He recalled his sense of anxiety and hope as he'd handed the bouquet to Sugiko earlier. Then he brought to mind the weight and feel of the flowers as they had been thrust back into his arms.

The next morning.

FLOWERS

Having finished getting ready to go to work, he paused in the middle of the room–briefcase in hand—and lowered his eyes to the desk. With one hand he extracted a single stem from the bouquet that lay there. His eyes took in the keen lines of the chrysanthemum's white petals, brimming with vitality as they had been the night before, while the innumerable leaves had withered and hung limp, wrapped around the stem like overly boiled spinach.

He gazed for a short time at the white flower, which raised its head loftily at the end of the stem. Grinding his teeth, he slowly forced open his lips. Suddenly biting into it, he gnawed half the flower away. Spitting out the petals that had swollen in his mouth, he muttered to himself, "Too nosy, am I?"

VOICE OF SPRING

春の声

Slipping an arm around Ishii's neck, Machida lifted him onto his back and threw him. He flew through the air, landing face up on the ground. . . . Dry, red earth showed through the sparse grass. His back covered all over with red soil, Ishii sprang to his feet at once, charging Machida. Face wet and shiny with sweat and tears, he ran toward Machida in his loose-jointed way, both arms flailing in wide circles. Even Machida was breathing hard and seemed to be having a tough time of it.

They'd been through the same cycle a dozen times in the last few minutes. Machida would throw him, and Ishii's body would float through the air and crash onto the ground. They both possessed thin, delicate physiques. They were city kids, sixth-graders at elementary school, and, whilst they were both weak, by nature they liked to run around.

On Sunday afternoon a quarrel broke out while they were playing on a vacant lot in the neighbourhood.

The cause was a trivial matter and, if anything, Machida had provoked it. It seemed he'd cooked up a pretext for a fight. It was a put-up job, so he could revel in the sensation he found so pleasant: hurling someone to the ground. For that purpose, Ishii was the only opponent at hand, everyone else being too tough for him to handle.

Yet again Ishii came at him, and Machida flinched. He realised Ishii's strength was starting to give out. Machida felt it was uncanny how Ishii could squeeze out one last ounce of strength when he oughtn't really to have had any energy left at all.

"What's this? Haven't you had enough yet?"

Silence . . .

"You crybaby!"

Despite what he'd said, Machida turned and fled. As it happened, he was the faster runner, and the distance between them opened up. When he stopped and turned around, Ishii was pursuing him in a leisurely manner, still with that loose-limbed running style, looking like he was about to pitch over. Ishii, running as if in a slow-motion movie, gradually loomed larger as he bore down on Machida.

Just then, Machida suddenly noticed something: Ishii's eyes were only half-open, and they weren't focused on him at all. Then he saw a look of pleasure spread almost imperceptibly across Ishii's face as he ploughed headlong into Machida's chest, his neck stretched out in front of him.

It seemed almost as if he'd consciously adopted a position that would allow Machida's arm to wind itself readily around him. Machida wrapped an arm around his neck, and the instant Ishii's body sailed into the air, the thought flashed across his mind, *I wonder if he needs me, too.*

Since Machida's strength was waning, Ishii didn't travel so far this time and instead collapsed to the ground, entwined about Machida's body. His arm still around his neck, Machida immobilised Ishii and looked down at his face immediately below. Ishii's eyes were slightly open. His wet face glistened, shining with some internal pleasure. The smell of grass came to Machida's nostrils.

"Hey, let's call it a day."

"No way," said Ishii, but he didn't try and push Machida away. On the contrary, letting the strength drain out of his body, he lay there, apparently enjoying the sensation of his back pressing against the ground with the weight of Machida bearing down on him from above.

"Let's stop now."

Machida began to get up, but Ishii tensed the arm caught up around him, trying to prevent him from pulling away. There was a peculiar elasticity about his strength, and Machida felt briefly dizzy. The dizziness passed in a moment, and he saw, close up, the single stem of a weed, as if it had been magnified.

Nearby the stem a small dragonfly, its wings looking as though they were coated in straw chaff, hung in the air, moving back and forth ever so slightly as if it were convulsing. It was a damselfly, often found drifting like this amid the grass.

Reflexively, Machida reached his hand out and made a grab at it. As if by some miracle, the damselfly, instead of skilfully avoiding capture as might have been expected, flew into his hand.

"Hey, I've caught it!" cried Machida excitedly, thrusting his loosely clenched fist in front of Ishii. In the middle of his fist a dry sensation ceaselessly tickled his palm.

"Caught what?"

Ishii's eyes were wide open. His misty, now half-open eyes disappeared finally, to be replaced by eyes with long lashes, like those of a young girl.

"A damselfly," said Machida, having stood up and now facing Ishii, who had gotten to his feet too. "I'll give it to you. Let's make it up and be friends again."

Whilst he felt the words 'make it up' didn't quite sit right with him, he held his fist out in front of Ishii. Ishii placed his fist against Machida's, as if to support it from underneath. Machida opened his hand slowly and deliberately, attempting to transfer the damselfly, but the moment his fist uncurled and slackened it slipped through his fingers and flew away.

"It doesn't matter. I don't like damselflies very much anyway," said Ishii, trying to console Machida, who was obviously upset at his failure.

Machida was fond of insects that were dry to the touch, insects that didn't look as though they would ooze if you squished them between your fingers.

"You dislike damselflies? Well, in that case, what do you like?"

If anything, his tone became reproachful and demanding.

"I like butterflies better."

"Butterflies? I don't, because they leave pollen on your fingers."

"The pollen's pretty."

"Pretty? So you like moths too?"

Machida assumed a slightly defiant attitude.

"Yeah, I like moths too."

"I hate them."

Ordinarily a quarrel would start from something like this.

Machida stared at Ishii's head. Slender and long, it had smooth skin. Then he would wrap an arm around his neck and send him flying. . . . Bringing to mind Ishii's partly-open eyes, for an instant Machida simultaneously felt both disgusted and excited.

He had an impulse to begin attacking him, but then he gave it up and let it go; he felt almost as if the scales of a moth were sticking to the tips of his fingers when he thought how Ishii needed him, too.

Machida looked at his own finger, in spite of himself. *Moth pollen? No, maybe it was butterfly pollen*, he thought.

Ishii's girlish eyes watched his actions circumspectly.

"I *really* like them," said Ishii, emphasising the point, his tone provocative.

Pretending not to have heard, Machida looked around the empty lot. Peering up at the sky, he checked the position of the sun.

"We still have some time before lunch. Let's go somewhere else," he suggested.

"Somewhere else? Where?"

"Your place would be good. Let's go to your house," he said, knowing full well that Ishii didn't like to invite friends to his home.

He hadn't said it to be annoying; it was simply that he wanted to go to Ishii's house. He persisted with his reluctant friend.

"You've an electric train set, right? Let's play with that, why don't we?"

It was true that Ishii possessed a variety of lavish toys. Machida was lying, though. He really wanted to see Ishii's sister.

Ishii's elder sister, Miki, was fifteen, but her good looks didn't belong to the world of children. And whilst she wouldn't hang around with them, if they were in the same house, just being able to feel her presence nearby was enough for Machida. Without waiting for a reply, he set off walking. They descended a small slope, climbed a narrow, steep incline and, when they came down the slope again, emerged in a cluster of stores. Ishii's house was still farther on.

Ishii stopped in front of a neighbourhood confectionery and called out, "Say, let's have a go at the lottery."

It seemed he was trying to delay arriving at his house for as long as possible.

Inside the gloomy interior was a young woman, sitting dressed in a kimono. She had a doleful, lonely face, but when she saw them she beamed. There appeared to be someone on the other side of the glass sliding door behind her. Through the glass they could see it was a middle-aged woman; the girl normally minded the store on her own.

Machida and Ishii picked out sealed pieces of paper from a box. Breaking the seals, they opened them and looked inside, but the papers were blank. You had to have the rubber-stamped impression of a sumo wrestler to win. If there had been the standing figure of a wrestler, the palms of both hands held out to the front at shoulder level and with the characters for *yokozuna* (champion wrestler) on his decorative apron, then they would have hit the jackpot.

All the pieces of paper they peeled open were blank.

"I give up," said Machida, holding his hand out to the girl tending the store. There was a gift even if you lost, and this store had made a special effort with its presents for losers. There had been a marked improvement since the girl started looking after the store about two weeks earlier.

Today, though, the girl just took two salted rice crackers out of a glass receptacle and placed them on Machida's palm. Turning her embarrassed gaze on Machida, who still held his hand out in unconcealed dissatisfaction, the girl lowered her eyes, letting her head droop without a word.

"Come on, let's go," said Ishii, pulling on Machida's arm.

"But . . ."

Machida started to say something, but in an uncharacteristically firm tone of voice, Ishii said, "It's alright, I tell you. Let's go. Let's go," and tugged even harder on his friend's arm. He felt intimidated by the girl with the drooping head and also by Ishii's strength; he was uneasy finding himself face to face with something so enigmatic.

Once they'd moved away from the confectionery store, Machida finally cooled off, asking, "But don't they usually give you more salted rice crackers? I mean, just giving us two like that . . ."

"We really only deserved two. The old lady who runs the store was there today, that's why. Usually the girl cheats on her and gives me extra. I think that's what happened."

"I get it."

Coming to a halt, Machida stared at Ishii in spite of himself. He felt like he'd been taken advantage of.

"You did well to notice, eh?"

"That girl—I'm sure she's divorced and moved back home. I know a lot about those kinds of things," said Ishii.

He seemed embarrassed rather than elated.

THEY DREW NEAR ISHII'S house, in the next district. Ishii commuted to an elementary school outside his neighbourhood. Occasionally they passed schoolkids with different cap badges from their own. For a moment, they would exchange glances, as if to gauge one another's feelings.

From the opposite direction, three boys walked towards them, carrying a bamboo basket. Judging from their height, they looked as though they were fourth-graders.

Stopping in front of them, Ishii called out, "Hey! Let me have a look at that basket, will you?"

He came across as friendly but at the same time menacing and confrontational. With his lean build, he was taller than all three of them and seemed more than capable of threatening them. One of the boys lifted the small basket up and showed it to him. Several green grasshoppers were in the basket, facing every which way.

"Give me one!"

The other stood there reluctantly without saying anything.

"Know them?" enquired Machida of Ishii.

"Nope," Ishii replied, a little haughtily. He stood tall, in an attitude that suggested he was going to take a grasshopper off this unfamiliar boy by force. With a weak adversary before him, he affected to be the neighbourhood bully. Machida had never seen Ishii behave this way before. It was exactly the sort of behaviour that he had shown toward Ishii, but now he felt he couldn't behave that way with him anymore.

Ishii knew he needed Machida, and so they went through the motions of colluding with one another, though, of course, it might have been a different story had they not been acting out their contrived roles.

"Know them?"

"Nope."

The boy carrying the basket put in, "I know all about it."

Ishii cast a hard look at him. Machida was unable to grasp what the kid was driving at, but Ishii's reaction was peculiar.

Suddenly Machida remembered something he'd heard. In a suggestive tone a classmate who'd gone round to Ishii's house to play had announced loudly in class one day, "Ishii's sister, you know, even puts makeup on her *you-know-what.*"

It was true that Ishii's elder sister often wore light makeup that wasn't in keeping with her age. Occasionally, she even wore heavy lipstick. He had always thought such spiteful comments were said in envy of her beauty, but now there was a link between what the kid had said and Ishii's manner. He didn't understand the answer yet, but Machida too felt strange.

"Hey, hand it over!" said Ishii, firmly.

"No way."

"Give it."

"We know about it," said the boy on the extreme left, in a teasing tone of voice.

In one violent move, Ishii wrested the basket from the hand of the kid in the middle.

"If you'd have handed it over quietly, I'd have taken just one bug and that would have been an end to it, see."

"Hey, are you taking all of them?" said Machida, in a low voice.

"That's right, I am," he replied, stubbornly.

The three boys mounted an attack in order to win back the basket, but the two of them—weak as they were—were enough to drive them away.

"I won't forget this!"

"I'm telling my brother on you!"

"You'll be sorry! Don't come crying to me later!"

Heaping abuse on them, the three kids ran off.

Ishii, at a loss as to what to do with the basket in his hand, just stood staring at it.

"I didn't want anything like this, do you realise?"

"Chuck it away then."

An unpleasant sense of foreboding stirred within Machida. He couldn't help feeling that now they had the basket there was more trouble in store for them. Ishii bent down and gently placed it at the side of the road. His customary litheness had returned to his movements, and, breaking into a trot, he distanced himself from the basket as though retreating from a bomb. Machida followed on behind, like he was being pursued by something.

They had probably put a hundred metres between themselves and the basket when they heard yelling coming from around the corner. The kids had commenced their retaliation with unexpected alacrity. The three of them appeared braced for a fight with the support of a young man—now taking the lead—who wore clogs on his feet and a white shirt billowing loose of his trousers.

The man's clogs rang out on the macadam road, and the lower edge of his shirt flapped about him. It seemed odd that the young man, who was clearly an adult, should be as excited as the children. Machida and Ishii fled for their lives, bolting away at breakneck speed. Turning into an alleyway, they sought refuge in a house at the far end; it was Ishii's house.

As they tumbled into the living room, two faces turned in their direction.

On that particular day, Ishii's elder sister, Miki, had painted her lips red, but Ishii's mother's face was even more heavily made up.

"What's going on? Coming flying in here in this rough manner . . ."

The two youngsters pricked their ears up for any sounds outside, strained expressions on their faces.

There was no time to reply.

"What's the matter?" repeated Ishii's mother. Her tone had changed from one of admonishing a mischievous boy to something rather more severe.

Just then, they heard the sound of confused footsteps running into the alleyway. In a moment, the signs of disquiet in the alleyway deepened and closed in on the front of the house.

"Come now, what on earth is going on?" the voice repeated, shriller.

As if in answer to that question, a shout gave up all at once outside the house, and when the battle cry had subsided, the children began to yell.

"*Oi*! Come out here!"

"Cowards. Come out right now!"

"This is what you get for picking on kids weaker than you!"

"Give up and come out, the pair of you!"

As they might have expected, they couldn't hear the young man's voice, but they could almost feel his raw gaze directed toward the house.

Worry lines had formed on Ishii's mother's forehead. Miki remained quiet, her eyes gleaming. Both hers and her mother's faces were beautiful. It seemed the presence of their faces was spurring on the young man.

The jeering outside gradually became louder.

"I hate it when strangers gather in front of the house like this. You should know that, shouldn't you? What on earth have you done?"

Her voice was frightened, trembling. Machida felt unable to stay there any longer. All of a sudden he was unbearably uncomfortable. There was a dark lustre in Miki's eyes, like some small, tender animal hiding deep in a cellar. But it wasn't a glimmer of fear.

What was it? wondered Machida.

Just then, the voices outside began shouting a new complaint.

"Come out, crybaby!"

What was the significance, he pondered, of kids from a different school knowing Ishii's nickname? Did it mean that the children—or perhaps even the whole neighbourhood—knew all about his family's affairs?

Just then, they heard an even louder voice.

"Come out, you little bastard!"

The voice was so loud because it had spoken with such boldness. And then, as if a dam had been breached, there began a deluge of similar words. It was the first time Machida had thought of Ishii in the context of what was being said of him. He recalled he hadn't ever seen Ishii's father.

Evening closed in, and Miki's red lips stood out in the gloom of the room, where they had neglected to turn on the lights.

"She even puts makeup on her *you-know-what. . . .*" The words of his classmates came to him now in a different light. Perhaps they'd intuitively figured something out.

Machida stood up. He no longer knew what to do. He could not stay in the house nor could he go outside. Inside the house was damp and cloying, while outside was, if anything, arid and inhospitable. Opening the door, he suddenly dashed out. Hoping that perhaps he could escape from the alleyway, he flew out like a bullet from a gun, but the brawny arm of the man barred his way. He seemed to be making an attack on the enemy's lines, and so the young man involuntarily applied an adult's strength with his arm.

OPENING HIS EYES, THE first thing Machida noticed was the yellow light of the electric lamp.

"Oh, good, he's come round!"

He'd been laid down in Ishii's living room. A damp towel pressed against his forehead.

"You tried to attack them for us, didn't you?"

Ishii's mother's smiling face looked down on him as he lay on his back. Her smile was somewhat distorted but brimming with kindness nevertheless.

So naïve, thought Machida.

Just then, he heard the very same words.

"He's so naïve, isn't he?" It was Miki's voice, but it had been directed at him. She went on, "Oh dear, I'm talking to him as if he's an adult, but he's still only a schoolboy."

Even she hadn't understood why he'd rushed out of the house, he reflected, but he said nothing. Miki remained silent, too. Her eyes were dark yet sparklingly defiant. While he was looking into them, he was struck by a new thought: perhaps he'd also been wrong about Miki. He was unable to explain why he'd dashed out of the house for fear that his very explanation would hurt her feelings.

And yet, even assuming one tried to hurt her, he wondered whether it would really have any effect, irrespective of whether it was he or that young man with the baggy white shirt. . . . Miki's painted red lips were a challenge to the world. She looked like a small, gentle, yet tenacious and beautiful wild animal.

A Bad Summer

悪い夏

Ichirō spent the summer with his two uncles, university students who had rented a room on the coast near a certain fishing village. They were brothers, and while their characters were somewhat different, they were both tall, well-built and cut dashing figures. The younger brother was flamboyant and had taken to painting a variety of novel pictures on his beach parasol. He dashed off paintings like a woman standing on her head with a shoe in the shape of a crown on her foot and a startled fish covered in spines.

"Quit painting such weird pictures, will you? It's embarrassing!" admonished the elder brother, but the younger remained unconcerned.

Ichirō, a fourth-grader in elementary school, was even more embarrassed than his uncle. He couldn't bear sitting in the shade of that beach parasol and hardly went near it.

He referred to his older uncle as "Big Uncle" and to his younger as "Little Uncle." When evening drew near, Little Uncle's daily routine was to swim out and dive off the springboard. As the sun approached the horizon, the surface of the expansive sea darkened, and the crests of the breaking waves began to turn a brilliant red.

As he leaped from the springboard his body made a graceful silhouette, describing all manner of forms in the air. He had carefully calculated the effect. Bending in two like a jackknife beginning to unfold, in the next instant he would stretch out taut, hands preceding his body as it sliced into the water; or he might flip several times in midair.

"Up to his old tricks again, eh?" said Big Uncle, standing on the beach and gazing on with a rueful smile.

Any number of young women hung around Ichirō's uncles. In the evening, several of them would invariably come over to their room. They would offer to play with Ichirō, who was always clinging to his uncles' sides. One evening, quite by chance, Ichirō discovered an amusing prank while playing with them.

One of the girls asked him, "Ichirō, would you like to ride on my back?"

Perhaps she was in the mood to half-tease Ichirō, who was at that in-between age where it was arguably inappropriate to ride around on a woman's back.

"All right."

Feeling a little playful, Ichirō climbed onto her back.

Burying his face in her luxuriant hair, a bittersweet odour stimulated something in the depths of his heart. A gentle resilience supported his body, and his hands, which hung casually over the girl's shoulders, brushed across the swell of her chest. Before he knew it, he was squeezing her breasts, a pleasant feeling rising up through his arms.

The girl suddenly screamed, and quite unexpectedly he was thrown from her back.

"Oh! You scared the life out of me!" he shouted.

"*You're* the one who scared *me!* You gave me such a shock!" laughed the girl, as she leaned over, her body almost bent in two.

From her tone and attitude, he figured she didn't really mind, so he decided he'd try it on the other girls, too, when the opportunity presented itself.

"Hey, give me a piggyback ride!" he would say, and the girl would unconcernedly turn her back towards him. Then there would be the same shriek, followed by the same peal of laughter.

They were like dolls that when touched about the chest had an amusing mechanism which produced a strange cry and the sound of laughter. Ichirō was taken by the feeling of manipulating those dolls, trying it out on one after another as they visited his uncles' rooms. Concealing his smiling face, he would ride on their backs, slowly extending his arms over their shoulders to revel in the mysterious palpitations he felt. Ichirō reflected that it was the same sense of vague apprehension he felt when coming face-to-face with a mechanical toy that acted unpredictably.

But the fifth girl responded quite differently. She promptly clawed his hands off and dumped him on the ground.

"You nasty brat," she snapped, glaring at him with sparking eyes.

Ichirō was startled. He'd never imagined he would be confronted by such a sullen, angry-looking face.

She was a slender-faced beauty, and Ichirō had thought her a mild-mannered, quiet woman. He was confused by her reaction, discovering a new and enigmatic fragrance in his play. He started to become aware that the mysterious palpitations he'd experienced so far were taking on new and different meanings. Ambivalent strands of thought deep within began to stir as a result, and he knew he'd stumbled across something important, something *real*, in his innocent games.

Ichirō's bad summer had just begun.

The name of the girl who'd glared at him naturally stayed with him. It was Takako. She was a young woman of about twenty. She wore a black swimsuit and was an excellent swimmer.

ONE AFTERNOON, ICHIRŌ WAS playing alone, making sand pies a short distance from the unconventionally decorated beach parasol. Lumping together wet sand into round shapes, he sprinkled them with dry sand to make two hard spheres. He dug out a conical depression, placed the two spheres alongside one another, then rolled them together into the hollow. One would break and crumble at the point where it collided with the other, and he quietly made a wager with himself about which would remain intact. He repeated his solitary game over and over again.

"Oh! What's this? Ichirō, are you playing alone?"

A winsome voice cascaded down from above. Looking up, he saw a pair of bright red painted lips. They belonged to a young woman called Kyōko, and next to her he saw Takako. Dazzled by the girls' presence, Ichirō felt a little self-conscious and uncomfortable.

"Ichirō, how about we challenge you to a game to see who'll win?" asked Takako affectionately, and, urging Kyōko on, they set about making sand spheres.

Kyōko spoke with a cloying, honeyed drawl as she always did, with her lips slightly apart. When her sphere collided with Ichirō's it shattered right away, but Ichirō could never defeat Takako's creations.

Suddenly a man's voice sounded above them as they crouched on the beach—a deep, resonant voice.

"Ichirō, how would you like to go out on a boat? I'm holding student swimming examinations now and I have to grade them."

The last part was spoken for the benefit of the girls. The man was an instructor at the seaside school. Ichirō recalled only having seen his face before, and it was the first time they had ever spoken. He was reluctant and glanced at the girls.

"You young ladies are welcome to come along, too. How about it? It'll be fun!"

He was a well-built, thirty-year-old man with close-cropped hair.

"I'm afraid I've got something I have to do, . . ." said Takako, her voice brittle.

"In that case, what about you, young lady? Won't you come along with Ichirō? Come on, let's go, Ichirō."

"Yes, why not? It might be fun to go out on a boat," replied Kyōko with a vague smile as she climbed into the boat with Ichirō, hurried along by the instructor.

The instructor moored the boat just off shore so he could score the students as they swam alongside. A sixth-grade class was taking the examination, and one by one the pupils swam by Ichirō, keeping a prescribed distance away from one another.

The instructor yelled powerfully, "That's good" and "Push your arms further to the rear!"

Ichirō was ill at ease. Even though the man was from another school, he felt uncomfortable being in a tiny boat with a teacher. He felt equally uncomfortable being present at the examination of boys who were ahead of him in school.

Kyōko started to feel bored. Shading her face with her hand, she squinted up at the dazzling summer sun and said in a loud voice as if to herself, "Oh! This is no good. I'll get sunburned."

Just then a youthful voice resounded in the distance.

"Hey! Kyōko! What are you doing out there?"

Looking up, Ichirō saw Little Uncle standing on the springboard about a hundred metres away, waving his arms madly.

"Oh dear!" exclaimed Kyōko in a low voice, and in the next instant she'd jumped into the water and was swimming toward the springboard with a graceful crawl.

"What the . . . ! How boring, left alone like this," muttered Ichirō.

"Ha, ha, ha!" laughed the instructor loudly. "Ichirō, why don't you go for a swim too?"

"It's a bit too far for me."

"Ha, ha! You ought to practice your swimming or something, instead of playing with girls all the time."

He bent over and scooped up a clump of brown seaweed from the surface of the sea close to the boat. Dozens of small, spindle-shaped, dark brown seeds clung to it.

Suddenly pressing the dripping wet weed into Ichirō's face, the instructor laughed again. "Ichirō, you must practice your swimming more," he scolded, scrubbing the mass across Ichirō's face.

He pressed it slowly at first and then with force. The scent of the ocean mingled with the smell of the seaweed assaulted Ichirō's nostrils. Just at that moment, he sensed another odour mixed in with that smell. Or perhaps it had emanated from the strength of the instructor's pressing hand—he wasn't sure which. It was that same dark, mysterious smell.

"Oh!" he cried.

The instructor pulled his hand away, turning aside with an unconcealed look of displeasure.

After that incident, Ichirō made it a point not to go anywhere near the seaside school, though before the summer was out he did happen to see the instructor just once more. It happened one evening. As he was passing beneath a cliff where the ruddy soil had been exposed he noticed the instructor sitting alone in a small restaurant nearby. Stooped over a wooden table, he was eating a reddish dish that looked like chicken fried with rice.

A TRAVELLING REVUE COMPANY had set up in a neighbouring fishing village, about four kilometres away, so one evening Ichirō, his uncles and four young ladies went to see a performance.

"Let's walk along the railroad tracks. It'll be much quicker," suggested Little Uncle.

"I'm a bit scared."

"Won't we get into trouble with the railroad people?"

The girls were against the idea, but then Kyōko said in a cheerful voice, "Come on, let's go. It'll be fun!"

Picking out the railroad ties with his feet, Ichirō hopped along the track one moment and the rails the next, arms held out to his sides as if he were walking a tightrope. The girls moved in single file along a narrow path parallel to the track. Grass hid the small ditch running alongside, and a damselfly flitted between the stems, its slim body like a twisted paper string.

"I love damselflies. They're not at all smelly," said Takako, reaching out a pale hand as if to catch it between her fingers.

"That's true. They don't stink, do they? I bet they'd be tasty sprinkled over rice and tea," said Big Uncle.

"It'd be tastier still to put the damselfly's eyeballs, boiled down in soy, on the rice and tea," said Little Uncle.

Kyōko snorted with laughter and said, "Oh! That's disgusting!"

Just then Ichirō saw Kyōko reach out and quickly pinch Little Uncle on his bare upper arm. Moving her fingers nimbly away, she swung her arms around in large circles, jumping into the thicket paralleling the railroad track and shouting, "Ichirō! I'll catch a damselfly for you."

"We can't stop in a place like this."

Even before Little Uncle finished speaking, a cry rose up from the middle of the thicket. "Ow!"

Kyōko raised an arm above her head and swung it round furiously. Several black objects hung from her fingertips, and she brushed them off with her other hand. They fell back into the thicket.

"Ow! Ow! There's still something on me."

In floods of tears, she clambered back up to the railroad track.

"What's the matter? Let me see."

Little Uncle grabbed her arm and raised her fingers up so he could have a look.

"Oh! It's bitten you, and only its head is left!"

TOWARD DUSK

"Just its head? Ugh, that's horrid! Get it off me!" Her voice had changed to a fawning tone.

Bending over her fingers, Little Uncle tried to remove the pea-sized insect's head. Kyōko brought her face close as well. Their cheeks almost pressed together.

"It's the head of a mantis. You were bitten by a praying mantis."

Little Uncle clapped Kyōko on her back.

By and by, the railroad led to a tunnel. It seemed to curve partway along, and they couldn't see the exit at the other end. The entrance gaped, like a pitch-black cave, and the girls stopped hesitantly in front of it.

"Come on. Let's keep going," said Little Uncle, in high spirits, but the girls continued to waver.

"Hey, Ichirō, you'll go through the tunnel, won't you?"

"Yeah, sure."

"*I'm* not going in there. It's black as night! It's dangerous!" refused Takako. Everyone stood at the tunnel entrance and looked about. They could see four or five children from the village hanging around in a field nearby. The lush silver grass, with its green ears, hid their legs from view.

One of the children was bending over, his body repeatedly disappearing and reappearing in the grass. The figures of the other children also bobbed about from time to time. The sun had begun to set, and all around was tinged with the hues of dusk.

"Hey! What're you doing over there?" called out Big Uncle to the children.

"We're making a grave for the cat."

"What happened to it?"

"It got run over by the train."

The girls swapped comments in subdued voices.

"He says it was run over right here! That's creepy."

"But would an animal as agile as a cat really get run over by a train, I wonder."

"Why, sure! Our cat committed suicide by jumping in front of a train," said Takako.

Little Uncle cut her short in a chiding tone. "Do you really think a cat would commit suicide? Cats are always in heat when they're run over by cars, you realise."

"Oh! They're in heat, he says. You're gross!" said Kyōko, trying to contain her laughter.

"It's not gross, it's the truth!" insisted Little Uncle, turning toward Takako, curiously taking what she'd said seriously. "When they're in heat, the cat's eyes become bloodshot and their vision gets dark and blurred. Then they get dragged under a car, and that's that."

"What? You don't even have a cat, and yet you suddenly seem to know all about it. Or did you work it out from your own experience?" said Big Uncle.

"What's that?" retorted Little Uncle testily.

"Idiot! You're supposed to laugh at that. There's something wrong with you."

Just then they heard a rumbling sound coming from inside the tunnel. The noise grew steadily louder until it became a deafening roar, and a locomotive sprang from the mouth of the tunnel, only a short distance away. They couldn't hear themselves think through the noise, and conversation stopped while the train passed.

As the din faded away, Takako said, in a tone that finally brought an end to the uncles' quarrel, "I'm not going through the tunnel. I'll go the long way round."

"Me too," agreed the other two girls.

"In that case, I'll go ahead, and I shall escort Takako," said Big Uncle.

"I'll go through the tunnel," said Kyōko, drawing close to Little Uncle.

"Good. Let's hurry up and go."

Still nestling close to Kyōko, Little Uncle began walking towards the tunnel but then stopped abruptly. Looking back at Ichirō, who was lingering behind, he asked, "Ichirō, you're with us, aren't you? Come on. Let's go."

Looking at the silhouettes of the men and women huddled close to one another and the gaping black hole of the tunnel behind them, Ichirō once again became aware of that dark, mysterious odour. That black tunnel entrance, which until now he'd thought nothing of, began to prey on his mind.

"Wait, Big Uncle! I'll go that way too."

"You will? Well, c'mon then, hurry up."

As if offended by what Big Uncle had said, Little Uncle put in, in a stubborn tone of voice, "You can't suddenly change your mind like that."

Then, catching hold of his wrist, he dragged Ichirō, who had drawn back, forcibly into the dark tunnel entrance.

As he walked through the tunnel, the high ocean waves of midsummer began to resound in his ears. The crashing surf, which must have been no louder than before, suddenly became deafening. Although the sea was close to the railroad track, it was hidden from view by low, grass-covered hillocks. Beyond the hillocks the sea suddenly swelled, towering, and Ichirō was seized by the terrifying illusion that the water would surge over the railroad track and engulf them.

On this day in particular Ichirō's mind continued to roil, unsettled, and the feeling remained with him even at the revue. A heavily made-up girl stood on the stage and gave a rendition of a popular song. She looked two or three years older than he, and when her voice hit a high note it invariably sounded reedy as it squeaked and cracked. Her voice triggered both disquiet and comfort in Ichirō.

Daybreak arrived as they made their way back. They decided to take the only two taxis in the village, both of which were jalopies, but one was already occupied. So all seven of them ended up squeezing into the other cab. Ichirō's two uncles, Takako and Kyōko sat in the back, more or less piled on top of one another. The other two girls squashed into the seat next to the driver.

"Hey, Ichirō, hurry up and get in here!"

From the half-lit seats, four faces turned in Ichirō's direction.

Ichirō froze at the spectacle.

"What are you doing? Get in quickly, will you!"

"But there's no room."

With his feet on the running board, Ichirō gripped the window frame and clung to the outside of the car.

"It's cooler outside. I'll ride out here."

"It's dangerous out there. You'll be thrown off!" cried Takako.

"I'll be alright."

Irritated at the delay, the driver pulled away. The instant the car began shaking over the bumpy country road, Ichirō suddenly felt he couldn't support himself. Flustered, he tried to climb into the cab through the window.

Realising what he was doing, Takako shouted, "Driver, stop! It's dangerous! You have to stop."

But the driver, taking no notice of her, merely sped up, and they dashed along the road.

Grabbing hold of Ichirō, who'd finally managed to get his head and shoulders through the small window, Little Uncle pulled him inside the car. Headfirst, he tumbled onto the laps of the four men and women sitting in a row, jostling one another.

He was embarrassed at how ungainly he must have appeared.

"You idiot! What a stupid stunt!"

Even as he heard Little Uncle's voice, the lips of Kyōko, who'd let out a giggle, rose up vividly out of the darkness. Those painted red lips rested lightly one on top of the other, their tips turned up tautly.

One evening several days later, Ichirō went to bed early suffering with diarrhoea, having become chilled during the night. A loud voice disturbed his slumber. Through the mosquito net he saw the silhouettes of his uncles standing facing one another on the veranda.

"You've no right to say such a thing," Little Uncle said.

"Perhaps. But then neither do you."

"It's up to Takako whether she accepts the way I feel about her, isn't it?"

"Yes, but what about Kyōko?"

"She's just a woman I see in the summertime," replied Little Uncle. "I really like Takako."

"You can't help who you fall for."

"Oh, what's this? You're talking almost as if you own her . . . ," said Little Uncle.

For a moment the conversation ended, but then the argument resumed, their voices suddenly hushed. Then Little Uncle unexpectedly let go a powerful jab.

"Oof!" A cry escaped from between Big Uncle's lips as he bent double, a hand held over his stomach. Before long he straightened up. "What the hell are you doing punching me?" he spat out.

Little Uncle stood a while in silence then suddenly turned about and vanished into the darkness beyond the garden.

Ichirō was wide awake. It was difficult to grasp what had occurred between his uncles, and with a slight irritation he once again sensed that dark and mysterious odour in the midst of the darkness. The sleep that finally carried him away was interrupted a second time in the middle of the night. Little Uncle had returned dead drunk but fell quiet before long, and Ichirō too soon drifted off to sleep.

In the morning, he heard something had happened at the beach during the night. A suspended log swing had been uprooted and lay on its side on the beach, and the changing rooms—a hut sheltered with reed screens—had been set alight and burned down.

"As they said, it's still arson, even if it was just a hut. The village police will probably look into it," said the village residents to each other.

Little Uncle stayed buried under his quilt and didn't get up for a long time.

In the afternoon another rumour circulated. In the hills close by the tunnel, the bodies of two lovers who'd committed suicide had been discovered. The incident had been reported by a villager who'd gone into the mountains to collect firewood. The police had gone to work on it right away. The couple looked as if they were from the city and didn't appear to have come here for the summer. They seemed to have taken a trip here, with that particular hill in mind.

A portable gramophone was found near the corpses, a record of a popular romantic song on the turntable. The rumour of the lovers' suicide promptly eclipsed gossip about the incident on the beach.

In the evening, walking alone on the seashore, Ichirō got into a scrap with five girls, probably sixth-graders from an elementary school, judging from their looks. As he was hanging around, the girls—whom he didn't recall having seen before—called out, teasing, "Oh look! He's walking around all on his own tonight! He's always playing with the girls, you know. Well, isn't that right, Ichirō? That's pretty strange, wouldn't you say?"

In that instant, the irritation, ambivalence and insecurity so pent-up over the last few days breached the dam all at once, swirling around within him.

For a fleeting moment he thought it odd that he found it so irritating, but then he went berserk, arms and legs flailing wildly at the girls. They put up a good fight, though, and when a passing grown-up caught Ichirō in his arms, he was covered all over with scratches.

The following day, the awkwardness between his uncles was gone, and Takako and Kyōko came over to see them as they always did.

But the end of the summer vacation was approaching, and the seaside became quieter with each passing day. When Takako, and later Kyōko, went home Ichirō accompanied his uncles to see them off at the station. Red and blue canna flowers were in bloom along the platform of the provincial station. Old fishermen with whom they'd become friendly also came to wish them a safe journey. They handed souvenirs through the train window: jars of honey when Takako returned home and a live octopus in a bamboo basket when it was Kyōko's turn to leave.

Big Uncle spoke mainly with Takako when it was time for her to return, and Little Uncle conversed mainly with Kyōko when it was hers.

Ichirō and his uncles began their own preparations to return to the city, and just at that time a sealed letter arrived addressed to Ichirō. The sender was an unfamiliar girl's name. Just by the seal was an elaborate drawing of a single, wide-open eye with long eyelashes.

The letter spoke of ordinary things, and from its content he realised the sender was one of the girls he'd quarrelled with the previous night at the beach. But, try as he might, he couldn't recall her face.

"What a boring letter," he muttered.

Big Uncle, who'd been peeking at what Ichirō held in his hand laughed, and said, "I bet the next letter that comes will have a single closed eye drawn by the seal."

Little Uncle put in, "Ichirō, she's fallen for you. No doubt about it." He laughed softly for what seemed like an eternity.

His laughing voice sounded strangely feeble.

Toward Dusk

夕暮まで

Chapter 1   At the Park

A LARGE BUS TRAVELLED along the single macadam road stretching straight into the distance, flanked on either side by expansive fields. Houses were dotted here and there, and before long the sea came into view. Gradually it grew nearer until the water's edge was directly beneath the road, breaking waves splashing white foam.

An area dense with houses appeared, obscuring the view of the sea, the road running through the middle. The smell of fish drifted into the bus. Having stopped twice, the bus again joined the road overlooking the sea before making a sweeping turn off left and slowly moving away from the coast. The fish smell disappeared. Most of the passengers had gotten off at the last two stops, and no one else had boarded. There was only a young woman left sitting in a seat right by the door and a middle-aged man sitting at the back. The woman stood, and, finding it a little difficult to keep her feet as the bus swung about, made her way to the seat at the rear. She sat down next to the man, and the female conductor glanced over, as if to say, "Oh, what's this?"

Until now they had been sitting apart, as though they were strangers. The woman was slightly built, almost like a young girl, and their ages were so different they could have been taken for father and daughter.

"You don't mind, eh? Now the stink of fish has gone," said the man.

"I'm sorry. It's not that I mind, it's just that . . ."

"I know, I know. You're right, it's better to take care. It'd be a nuisance for you if people gossiped."

Several of her friends lived in the seaside town the bus had passed through a little while earlier, and the woman had been afraid of being seen. They weren't the sort of couple who would attract attention even if they had talked to one another, but now that things had come this far, they were unable to rid themselves of the feeling of watching eyes. The suspicious atmosphere surrounding them drew the curious gaze of the conductor.

The yellow interior lights came on. Sundown was approaching, although it was still faintly light outside the window. No sooner had the bus turned its lights on than it arrived at the last stop. Although it was the terminus, there was no town or garage there.

Without picking up even a single passenger, the bus slowly turned around and sped away. The two were left quite alone, a stretch of flat land in front of them. The ground ended in a cliff about three hundred metres ahead, and beyond that the sea, having disappeared once, revealed itself again.

"Is this the sort of place you had in mind? Is it a park?" asked the man.

"Yes, this is what I was thinking of."

"There's no one about. I wonder why the bus comes all the way out here."

"It'll be busier come the summer. Would you prefer to be in a crowded place?"

"No, it's better if nobody's about."

It was dusk, yet the sky wasn't orange. Clumps of trees scattered here and there on the flat ground appeared a dirty grey.

The area overlooking the cliff had been turned into a park, and the concrete gate and railings in front of them were the same dirty grey. The sea, too, was dark grey, though the colour was lustrous: the whole park back-lit against the faint light.

The layer of light purple haze covering the ground felt like a slight discharge of electricity playing on his skin, thought the man. It was as if they had wandered into a different world.

"But tell me, why did you fancy coming to a place like this?" asked the woman.

"No reason in particular."

"I wonder if anyone would really go to the trouble of taking the bus here for no reason."

"I wanted to drive, but you said we had to come by bus."

"That's true, but . . ."

"Whenever I see you, we end up in a room somewhere. We can't keep our hands off each other. Then we always do the same thing, every time—it was getting a little tiresome."

"It's a little late to say that. Thanks to you, Sasa-san, I can't get married now."

"Sasa-san? That's pretty formal."

"That's what you want, isn't it? That's why we've come all the way out here, isn't it? But it's too late. You're the first man I've been with, and now I can't get married."

"That's an old-fashioned thing to say."

"It's not old-fashioned. It's the truth! Everyone deludes themselves. Men, and women too."

"If you can't deceive yourself, you can deceive the other person—you know, the man you'll end up marrying."

"Is that all you think about, deceiving people?"

Her voice was full of loathing, and he shot a quick glance to see her expression.

"Anyway, let's go inside. We're here now after all. It'll soon be nightfall," said the woman, still facing forward.

Twilight turned to dusk, and the outline of the park gates and railings seeped through the darkness. The light purple haze filled the space as before, and he could clearly see the woman's face and even her expression. They went through the park gates, seeing no sign of a gatekeeper. A path ran straight from the gates to where the ground petered out, its macadam surface emerging pale in the darkness. Other than that, there were just some clumps of trees dotted about on the flat ground.

"Shall we try walking to the end of this path?" he asked, and they set off walking side by side.

Although an unenclosed place, their shoes striking the macadam surface gave off a muffled echo. The sky had turned almost completely black, but the light purple haze—three times the man's height—covered the ground as before. The expanse gave the illusion of walls and a ceiling from which sound rebounded.

As they walked slowly along, the man said, in a disinterested voice, "I had an unpleasant dream."

The woman said nothing.

After a moment's hesitation, he continued, "You were walking along crying, holding hands with a woman I've never seen before. You were both wearing black boots. The woman didn't try to console you, but instead simply walked along holding your hand, with a pale expression. You were the one crying. One side of your face was red and pulpy, like a crushed, ripe persimmon."

The woman continued to walk a while in silence.

"The woman you're talking about—she wasn't tall, with puffy eyelids, was she?"

"Yes, she was."

"Maybe what you saw wasn't a dream."

"What nonsense."

"It's just that you said things like her face was red, like a ripe persimmon. Your dream was in colour, wasn't it?"

"There are colours in my dreams. Even down to the neutral tints."

"Oh, of course, there are dreams in colour. But that wasn't a dream. I walked about like that once before, you see."

As she spoke, she raised her left hand and covered the left half of her face with her palm. The man walked even with her, to her right. The sky had turned completely black, but the colour of the air encircling them if anything imparted an even lighter glow than before, and her actions were quite clear to him.

The man recalled a certain ghost story.

Midway down a slope, he passed a male goblin without eyes, a nose or a mouth. Shocked, he ran to the bottom, where there was a noodle stall. He piled into the stall, and, when he spoke about what he had just seen, the old man in the stall grinned, and said, "Did that man you're talking about look like this?" *Sliding one hand down over his face, he revealed a blank, with no features whatsoever. . . .*

He looked for a reaction in the woman by his side.

"My face was like this, was it?" she said, removing her hand. The left half of her face was red and crushed to a pulp. But that didn't really happen, and she walked away with her hand still held against her face.

Irritated, the man said, "It was a dream, for sure. That much is obvious."

"Why is it obvious?"

"Because I saw it myself, so I'm certain it was a dream."

"I wonder if that's right."

Irritated by her sceptical tone, he said, "I can prove it was a dream."

"You can prove it?"

"You were both walking along naked. So it had to be a dream."

"In that case, we wouldn't have been wearing black boots, would we?"

"You were wearing boots. Apart from that you were stark naked," said the man, deliberately intending to shock.

"Even so," the woman muttered furtively, "I wonder if that's right."

They reached the end of the path. Railings had been erected at chest height, and beyond that was the cliff. They could dimly make out the black sea below and the white spray from the crashing waves. He took hold of the woman's forearm and steered her in the direction from which they had come. The pale path ran straight to the distant exit gate.

Leaning back against the railing, she said, "When you dream, your eyes are closed, right?"

"That goes without saying."

"But what does it mean to close your eyes?"

"What do you mean, 'What does it mean?'?"

"Your eyelids come down and cover your eyeballs, right?"

"I suppose so, if you put it like that."

"If that's so, then your eyeball is always left open."

"I see. In the past there were philosophers who wrote about that. Even when your eyes are closed, your eyeball is left open, so you're always looking at the inside of your eyelid. There isn't a moment's rest. It's a fairly neurotic way of thinking, you know."

"Staring at the flesh on the back of your eyelids. Come to think of it, that's just what it is, isn't it? But that's not what I'm thinking. You close your eyes, right?" said the woman, demonstrating by shutting her own eyes. Her appearance became increasingly distinct to him. It was dark round about, and only the area immediately surrounding them was illuminated in light purple.

"I put my hand in front of my eyes like this." She placed the palm of her hand over her closed eyes, spreading out her five fingers. "You can clearly see the outline of your fingers through your eyelid."

"That's neurotic too."

"Oh? It's not just me, you know. Anyone can see it, of course."

"Don't be ridiculous."

"Go on, try closing your eyes."

The woman extended her palm in front of the man, who had his eyes closed.

"You can see, right?"

"Why should I be able to see?" he began. The outline of five fingers came indistinctly to his eyes, the image coming into focus bit by bit, and then the outline stood out in strong relief. He couldn't see the patterns on her fingertips or the lines on her palm, but he could make out the shape of her hand as if it had been cut out from a sheet of white paper.

"Oh, . . ." he murmured.

The woman's voice was lugubrious, if anything. "You can see it, can't you?"

"Yes."

"You can even see my face."

She seemed to move her face in front of his closed eyes. He could see it distinctly. He could even see her features. It got so that he couldn't tell if his eyes were open or closed. He tried touching his fingertips against his eyelids and found they were closed.

"Don't worry. Your eyes are shut."

He heard her voice. The other parts of her were like a white cutout from a sheet of paper and threw up the outline of her body in sharp relief. She appeared to be naked.

"Is this what I saw? I wonder," he murmured, in spite of himself. When he opened his eyes, the woman was right in front of him, fully clothed. He thought she was perhaps the woman he had seen with his eyes closed, walking about crying with half her face red and crushed.

Perhaps she knew what he was thinking, and she said, "There is a way of telling whether it is a dream or reality."

"Tell me what it is," said the man meekly, though he was still irritated.

"For example, if among the scenes you see in your dream your own face or back appears to you, then that is a dream." A glimmer flashed in her eyes, as though she were mocking him. "Maybe you're too old to understand that kind of thing."

She reached out and stroked his stomach. He had become quite corpulent around his midsection. The woman leaned back against the railing again and stared at the pale path that ran to the gate as if measuring its length with her eye. "I'll race you to the gate." Her tone had become challenging.

"You can't beat me!"

The moment he finished speaking, she began to run. Flustered, he took off after her.

She was already ten metres or so ahead of him, and the gap wouldn't easily be closed. Suddenly, the clothes disappeared from her body, and her white nakedness greeted his eyes. As he ran, the man raised one hand and checked his eyelids, but they weren't closed.

"They're open," he murmured. Just then, a red liquid flowed from between the woman's thighs. It streamed ceaselessly as she ran, staining her legs a deep crimson.

The man knew he had to catch up and stop her, and just at that moment her legs gave out and she stopped in a crouch. From where she was squatting on the surface of the pale path, her naked back bent double, she turned only her head and looked back at him. A flirtatious, alluring look appeared, and in a moment it had spread across her face. As before, the red liquid coursed from between the woman's legs. The pale surface of the path where she crouched was stained red. Gradually the pool spread, but her expression remained the same. The man came to a standstill about three metres distant, uncertain whether to approach her or turn around and leave.

His indecision was apparent in his slightly stooped back. The shoulders of the man's own back—that uncertain back—bent around the contours of its protruding shoulder blades, met his eyes clearly.

Chapter 2   Caught in a Net

THERE WAS A SMALL Western-style restaurant on the outskirts of the shopping quarter. A single-storey timber building, it was known simply by its old-fashioned name, 'Western restaurant.'

About five years before Sasa had been told by a friend that the steak there was delicious. "But whatever you do, don't leave the fat!" his friend had added. "The old guy that runs the place got mad at me for leaving some the other day."

The back of Sasa's head had started to itch. He dug his nails in and scratched vigorously.

"You don't fancy it?" his friend had asked, eyeing him.

"He sounds a bit fussy."

"Not really. He always brings the dishes to the table and then just goes right back to the kitchen without a word. I've been there plenty of times. Maybe it's a sign I've become a regular," said his friend with a thoughtful expression, but he didn't press the matter further.

Sasa decided to give it a try. There were only stores with show windows in this neighbourhood: stores displaying brilliantly coloured kimonos, specialty stores with just two or three pairs of sandals, stores displaying rows of variously coloured and shaped bottles of wine and spirits, and the like.

The restaurant, with its weathered, dark-grey siding, resembled the entrance to a cave, but the white cloth curtain with only its name written on it in India ink was neat and clean. Four tables had been arranged in the small rectangular restaurant, and there were only three items on the menu: soup, steak and crab croquettes. The kitchen, though, was spacious. The restaurant was run by an obstinate-looking, slightly built, gaunt old man and an old woman, who seemed like a female version of him; other than that there were no staff.

The steak was delicious. The restaurant wasn't busy; before long, a group of customers who had been there before him left, and as Sasa stood up another group came in. They seemed to be regular customers in their twos and threes, but the owner didn't pass the time of day with them. Nobody was ill at ease. If anything they were used to one another's ways. . . . The place seemed to have come into being like an air pocket in the busy shopping quarter.

Sasa took to visiting the restaurant when the mood struck him. While the owner always greeted him with a cold expression, he didn't make him feel unwelcome.

ONE DAY SASA TOOK Sugiko with him. He vaguely imagined the owner would openly reveal his disgust at an older man accompanied by a young woman, but as it turned out he welcomed them with a rare smile. Perhaps he had mistaken Sugiko for the daughter of one of Sasa's relatives.

If anything, his smile made Sasa feel all the more uncomfortable.

As Sasa lit a cigarette, the meal having finished, he dropped his lighter on the floor. Bending over to retrieve it, a flat bottle of olive oil slipped out of his inside pocket. The side of the bottle hit the wooden floor with a loud clatter. Feigning indifference, he picked the bottle up and put it back in his pocket. Then, pursing his lips, he made a face.

"Oh, please," Sugiko murmured. The florid colour around her throat spread until her entire face was flushed peach-blossom pink. Her complexion returned to its normal pallid colour shortly, and she added, "I hate it when you do things like that."

Her tone of voice belied a complex blend of embarrassment and disgust; yet there was a hint of sweet naivety there also.

— 134 —

Not having expected anything like that to happen, she was at a loss.

Could they really say there was a sexual relationship between them? Sugiko would always close her thighs tightly together to prevent anything from happening. Dripping olive oil into the tight seam between her adolescent thighs and pressing himself against her, he was able to achieve more or less the same sensation. But Sugiko was still a virgin.

Leaving the restaurant, he noticed a kimono in the window of the store next door. It looked to him like bridal attire. He stopped briefly, as if to conceal the window, and then began to walk again. Cutting down a narrow lane flanked on either side with stores, they came out on the main street.

There was a drugstore on the corner to the right. Coming to a halt nearby, Sasa placed a hand over his midriff and muttered, "My stomach's a little upset. I wonder if I should buy some medicine."

"You're going to buy it from that store? You go in there a lot, don't you?"

"Why do you say that?"

"It's where you bought the olive oil earlier, isn't it?"

"Oh, so that's it. You blushed when I dropped the bottle on the floor."

"But . . ."

"You looked really cute. Nobody would connect olive oil with *that*, I tell you. After all, people use it so they tan evenly, don't they?"

There was no sign of any suntan on Sugiko.

"If you say so. It's autumn, you realise." Letting the words slip out like a sigh, she looked up at the sky. Enticed, Sasa tilted his head back too. It was September. The sky had turned autumnal blue.

When he had first met her, Sugiko had had a dark tan. It had seemed to him as though the scent of perspiration and the ocean lingered behind her ears. A year had gone by since.

"Speaking of which, you didn't go to the seaside this year, eh?"

"I meant to go, but I couldn't. It was your fault, Sasa-san."

"My fault? What makes you say that?"

"Last year's swimsuits are all no good. I can't squeeze into any of them."

Bashfulness and coquetry passed faintly across her face.

"Why don't you buy some new ones then?"

"People back home will think it's strange—you know, that in just a year my hips have gotten so big."

Sugiko's parents were in good health, and he'd heard she had two elder brothers. Not that he'd paid much attention to that, although he couldn't guarantee there wouldn't come a time when he would need to talk with her folks.

"Could my hips have gotten so big just by doing *those* kinds of things?"

"It's a shame you weren't able to swim, isn't it?"

His words had an insincere ring to them.

"I don't mind. I can't swim in any case," said Sugiko, simply.

"But I thought you could."

"I can swim in the sea, but . . ."

"In the sea? I don't get it."

Ignoring what he'd said, she continued, "I need something to hold onto, you see. And it has to be something decent, something publicly acceptable."

Sasa felt as if he were an inadequate black stick floating on the surface of the water.

He stood there without saying anything.

"I wish I was good at something. If only I were," sighed Sugiko.

It occurred to Sasa that perhaps she was thinking that if only she could protect her virginity she'd get along somehow. It would make up for not being able to stand on her own two feet.

"Are you catching the train now?" he said, serious all of a sudden.

He could see the National Railways platform lit up in the distance. He'd left his car in a nearby car park.

"Well, . . ." began Sugiko, snuggling close.

Sasa had been aware for several months now of her increasing femininity. She'd seemed boyish when they first met.

Occasionally, she'd smelled faintly of sweat, and that had fanned his sexual desire and at the same time stirred within him a slight sense of disgust.

"I like the restaurant we went to just now," she said.

It was probably because it was a low-key place, thought Sasa, but he didn't say anything.

"The meat was delicious," she said, adding, "I like good food."

"So, are you going home?" said Sasa, turning his gaze toward the platform, suspended like a belt of light under the low night sky.

Putting her hand lightly around his arm, Sugiko didn't reply.

SEVERAL MIDDLE-AGED MEN HAD been invited to the young couple's party.

He had known the host's ulterior motive was to have the men pay when the youngsters ran out of money, but he had gone along with it even so.

Sugiko, whom he had met for the first time at that party, looked about eighteen at the time.

"You look like a kid. But you must be about twenty-two, right?" Sasa had said.

"That's the first time an older guy has managed to guess my age," she had replied, looking directly at him.

A woman who introduced herself as Yūko cut in, "Sugi's a virgin, you know."

"Really?" he had replied, dubiously.

"Boys are afraid and don't go near her."

"How come?"

"Because she's always going on about having a beautiful wedding. You know, all that talk about a white dress and everything."

Sugiko had drunk several whiskys. It looked like she could hold her drink; her face wasn't flushed and her eyes were clear.

It was Mieko who had invited Sasa to the party. He'd been seeing her on and off for about a year.

"I wonder if I should try asking that girl Sugiko out," he had said to her.

"Well, you could try, but I wonder if it'd work out."

"Yeah, you said that before."

"But, you know what? She eats a lot," said Mieko, indicating Sugiko with her eyes.

Mieko was the same age as Sugiko.

The night Sasa had invited Sugiko out for dinner he had right away driven his car into the basement car park of the hotel. Without making any effort to get out of the passenger seat, Sugiko had said, "Where are we?"

"You know where we are. That's why you're clinging to your seat."

"So, what I'm trying to say is, I don't want to."

"Why don't we just take a peek at the room?"

It seemed her curiosity had got the better of her, and maybe she wondered what would happen if they did. She got out of the car. Sasa drew close to her, something her young male friends wouldn't even try to do. There was something about her that suggested she'd been waiting for an older, more confident man like him to make a move.

Sasa ran his hands over her body as if he were slowly peeling a layer of skin, and it took hours before he was finally able to expose her breasts. They had to make endless visits to hotel rooms before he could persuade her to shed all of her clothing.

It took him two months. Even after she was naked, she was reluctant to give herself completely to him.

Clamping her thighs firmly together, she wouldn't allow Sasa's fingers to come near. Yet, curiously, she didn't mind him using his tongue; she knew his tongue wouldn't rupture her hymen.

It was almost too easy. Afterwards, though, she went into the bathroom and vomited. Sasa assumed her membrane had ruptured.

While all of this was going on, one day Sugiko suddenly started using her lips and her tongue. Her movements were adroit from the beginning, though it wasn't something Sasa had taught her. Bringing her naked body close to him, she buried her face deeply in his chest. But as their torsos came together, a look of fear suddenly came into her eyes and her body stiffened, as it had before. From time to time, that stiffness left her and she would let out a cry, like a sigh, and raise one of her arms high in the air. Sasa applied his lips to that hairless armpit and tried to penetrate her, but it was impossible. That moment vanished like a break in a thick layer of clouds, and Sugiko's body became rigid again.

ONE EVENING, WHILE SASA was talking with a guest in the reception room, the telephone rang.

He heard Mieko's voice at the other end. "Guess where I am right now?"

"I've no idea."

She mentioned the name of a large hotel in the city centre. She was probably trying to lure him out, he thought; occasionally he had had calls like this from Mieko, though he'd never once phoned her. Conscious that he was within earshot of his visitor, he said, "That sounds wonderful."

Then she said something he wasn't expecting: "Do you know who I'm with?"

Ah, that's why she called me, he thought, realising his misunderstanding. "It must be your boyfriend."

"Not my boyfriend. My fiancé."

"Oh, well pardon me. You're in bed now, I guess."

"I am. But he's in the bathroom."

"Well, it sounds even more wonderful. What can you see from the bed?"

Sasa reverted to the tone he always used when talking with Mieko on the phone. Only his manner of speaking was more courteous than usual.

"The sky," she replied.

"I see. The sky, eh?"

"I can see the sunset. The clouds are beautiful."

"What is it you wanted to say?"

"Nothing. I just fancied talking to you."

"Just fancied talking? Listen. I'm a little busy right now."

"Oh, well pardon me. Some other time then."

She hung up.

"I'm sorry about that. Some people just won't stop babbling," said Sasa to his guest, with a forced laugh.

Most of the young men and women in Mieko's circle were what you might call good kids from respectable homes. But Mieko's family was a little different. It seemed her father didn't live with them, and they didn't appear to be that well off either. Even before she met Sasa, Mieko had been with the young man she called her fiancé. Sasa doubted the man saw their relationship the same way she did. He seemed to be the type who wanted to make an advantageous marriage, but Mieko didn't appear to be worthy of his attention. And yet, for all that, the guy didn't want to let Mieko go. When that sense of insecurity got the better of her, she would call him and they would end up going together to a hotel.

What was the call just now all about? he wondered.

The following afternoon she phoned again. The first thing she said was, "Yesterday I had a terrible time. He left me tied

— 140 —

to the leg of the bed all night, naked, with my hands fastened behind my back."

"But why?"

"There was a phone in the bathroom too. When I was talking to you, he could hear every word."

"I don't think it's anything to worry about, even if he did hear."

"He said that made it all the more suspicious. He said I must have a really close relationship with you. He demanded to know who you were and really laid into me."

"He did?"

"But I didn't tell him. I just said it wasn't that sort of relationship. He likes to pick fights and tease me over the slightest things."

"There are guys like that."

"How about it, Sasa-san? Why don't we get together?"

"What was yesterday's call all about?"

"I was happy, that's all."

"I see. But you were up all night. You must be tired."

"I don't mind really."

"It's great to be young, eh? I pretty much worked through last night, too."

"Oh, a guy in that state is kind of aggressive. It turns me on."

"I know you know all about it. But I'll have to say no today. Look me up again another time."

At times like this Mieko was straightforward. "OK. Next time then!"

It seemed to be the end of the call, but suddenly Sasa didn't want to hang up. With the fatigue of being up all night, he didn't feel much like going out. Had Mieko been there with him, he'd have felt like getting right into bed and playing around a little. That way his tension would gradually dissipate, and he'd probably be able to get off to sleep. If the call ended now, he'd still be stressed.

"Wait a minute. Won't you talk to me a bit longer?"

"What do you want to talk about?"

"I just want to chat. About how many guys have you slept with?"

"Oh, what's this? Does it bother you?"

"No, no. I'm just asking."

"I'd like to say you're my second, Sasa-san."

"Oh? Then that would make him your first."

"That's right. He's my first."

"And yet, why have you had so many after him?"

"I wouldn't say it's so many."

"But you easily allowed me into your circle of friends."

"He taught me all this. He did some surprising things right from the start. But back in those days he was gentle."

Sasa grew weary. "It's all a bit difficult, isn't it? I've gotten sleepy."

"And now you've suddenly become tired of me. Doesn't bother me! Let's ring off now."

She hung up.

Sugiko lay on her back, fully stretched out. Her legs were firmly clamped together, arms glued to her sides. Sasa dripped olive oil into the hollow of her groin between her tightly shut thighs and laid his body over hers. It was a risky situation for Sugiko to be in. She refused to create a gap between her legs, and Sasa did not try to prize them apart. When it came down to it, he wasn't able to marry her.

Before long, Sugiko grew accustomed to this position and came to think it was safe. For six months they continued doing it this way. Occasionally, he tried to force her legs apart, but immediately became flaccid.

Sasa too was afraid. Still, could it really be said that Sugiko was a virgin? Technically, she might have been, and he tried hard to understand how she felt about it.

Even now he didn't know how she behaved with her friends. Sometimes there were vivid burn marks on the backs of her hands and around her wrists.

"This is really bad, don't you think?"

She would happily raise her arm and indicate the marks with her eyes.

"What happened?"

"Someone pressed a lighted cigarette against my arm when we were out drinking."

A cigarette stubbed out on the back of her hand. The smell of scorched skin lingering ever so slightly. Sasa could picture the scene: Sugiko, far from attempting to avoid it, presses her hand against the lighted tip. This suggested she had a masochistic streak, all the more reason to conclude she was a twenty-two-year-old virgin.

Lying on top of her, he whispered vulgarisms in her ear. "Go on, say it," he urged.

She quietly mimicked him, and then, after a few seconds, she tilted her head backwards and let out a loud scream, her voice a blend of shame and excitement. The exposed skin on her neck was angry and red.

Then Sasa began to lose control over his desires, and in an utterly unemotional voice, Sugiko cried out in pain and told him to stop.

Faced with that verbal onslaught, Sasa lost his erection.

He and the people in his crowd used a number of hotels that catered especially to lovers. It was the first time he'd been to the hotel they were using that night, and once there Sugiko began to shout her refusal over and over. Before long, they heard a hotel staffer inserting a key in one of the doors. There was a small room beyond the partition with a table and chairs and a refrigerator. The door to that room opened, and Sasa sensed someone was there. Patting Sugiko on the cheek, he motioned in that direction. Her eyes were still shut, but she immediately

— 143 —

fell silent, the expression on her face remaining as it had been while she was shouting.

For the first time, Sasa saw a faint smile cross her face.

Some women smile when they are with a man. The smile is sweet, tender and then captivating. The pleasure illuminates the woman's face from deep within: a moderate, soft smile. At that moment, all that is in a woman's heart is the sexual desire to nestle close to the man. And then before long the smile reveals an even deeper pleasure.

Sugiko's smile was different. It resembled a look of ridicule, but she didn't appear to realize it. Eyes tightly shut, her entire body was taut with energy, a response to an as-yet-unfamiliar stimulus and a resistance to Sasa's persistent advances. From between those two contradictory emotions both self-contempt and ridicule emerged, and Sugiko wore them lightly on her face in an expression that was almost a smile. That smile withered Sasa's erection even further.

The person in the adjoining room was still there and seemed to have an ear turned toward the bedroom. They could sense the person's presence, although whoever it was didn't call out to them.

Sugiko remained silent, and the room was quiet.

"Is something the matter?" Sasa called out.

"No. I've just come to check the refrigerator," came the voice of a middle-aged woman.

They heard the door closing, and the woman disappeared.

"You were too loud. She probably thought you were being raped."

"But . . ."

"She won't come back. And now we're alone again, I'm going to rape you for real!" he said, and as he started to bear down on her she let out a long scream.

A faint smile surfaced again on her face; he could imagine her wearing it with a nonchalant shrug after playing a prank on someone. This time she was conscious of it, and she seemed to have forced the smile. Still with his failed erection, slight feelings of hatred stirred within Sasa.

WHENEVER SHE MET SASA, Sugiko demanded they spend time over a leisurely meal. They'd got into the habit of doing this before going to a hotel.

One evening, about a year after they'd first met, Sugiko and Sasa were in a basement restaurant together. Tables had been arranged randomly about the spacious floor, and most of them were occupied.

Sasa paused and turned his gaze on Sugiko as she ate her fillet of sole, sautéed meunière style. Manipulating her knife and fork skilfully, she separated the flesh from the bones. He stared at her thinking she must have been raised in a fairly well-to-do household which, if anything, he found all the more tiresome. Sugiko's friend Yūko was three or four years her senior, lived alone and supported herself. It seemed she'd been brought up in a different sort of environment.

Yūko had once said to Sasa, midway through their conversation, "Oh, yes. Do you know about Sugi's photo collection? It's famous. I'm talking about those pictures she has of men and women."

At the time, Sugiko was twenty-three, and Sasa had been keenly aware that even at that age she was still a virgin.

As they finished dessert, he put his hand in his inside pocket, pulled out a fistful of colour photos, and without warning thrust them in front of her. Pictures of foreign men and women in suggestive poses were clearly printed on the photos. Sugiko's head jerked down obliquely, as if she'd been slapped. Sasa returned the bundle of photos to his pocket right away, though he couldn't be certain the people sitting round about hadn't seen them too.

"Stop it," said Sugiko, her face colouring.

"Yūko said you have a collection."

"But in a place like this?"

"You got a kick out of it, didn't you? Your eyes are all wet."

They left the restaurant. At the hotel room Sugiko demanded, "Show me those photos."

She looked eagerly at the photos he'd taken out of his inside pocket. They were playing cards made in Sweden, each with a different colour photograph. Various designs had been used; for instance, in the picture on the Five of Hearts, five men and women were intertwined. There was no hint of perversion, and in some of the pictures the people appeared to be enjoying sports. It was like a practical demonstration of various postures, and all were devoid of any feverish enthusiasm, erotic perversion, shame or obscenity.

Sugiko, looking eagerly at each card in turn as she lay face-down on the mattress, began sorting them into piles, commenting "I like this card, but not this one."

Sasa looked from her hand to the photos.

"This is amusing." She placed the joker to the left side of her bed. The card showed a black man's and a white man's penises, thrust horizontally from left and right, their tips pressed against each other.

The purply black and blood-suffused red were bonded and looked like a single stick dyed red and black. A woman with short hair, like that of a young girl, was doing her best to take it into her mouth with her lips around the join. Her face was angelic.

The female models were all beautiful. One of them, a platinum blonde, had adopted the posture of a beast. A powerfully built white man knelt behind her and scooped her waist up with both arms from the rear. On his left upper arm he had an indigo-coloured tattoo of an eagle. With her neck bent back and her 'forepaw' extended in the posture of a howling animal, she took another penis from the front deep into her mouth.

Sugiko hesitated for a moment before placing the card to the right. But she was in no doubt about placing the card with the design of the combination of one man and two women on the pile to the left. The man stood holding a woman tightly in each arm, and the youthful, taut lines running from the back to the hips of the women formed beautiful arcs to the left and right. In the space thus created between the left and right curves was a towering arrow.

Then there was a picture of a long, thick rod, blood vessels bulging in relief, extending horizontally, such that the card was divided equally top and bottom, with the moist, red tongue of a woman applied to its tip.

A gentle, tender and loving expression floated on the woman's well-contoured profile. Another woman was facing forward and holding that large penis sideways in her mouth. Her expression suggested she was slightly distressed on account of opening her mouth so wide, and one could see a narrow gap between her barely visible white front teeth.

On another card on top of a recumbent woman lay another woman, her body pressed snug against the curve of her body. And on top, a large man lay over both of them.

Teeth bared, a black woman and a white woman bit into a man's shoulder, one on each side of him. The man's chest and stomach were dense with stiff, tangled hair.

Sugiko's nimble fingers sorted all of those cards into the left-hand pile. Then her fingers paused in the air. "I wonder what this is."

Her eyes were moist as she looked at Sasa. The card showed a close-up of a woman's genitals taken from behind. Her vertically aligned orifices were pierced through by two sturdy lengths of flesh.

"I sometimes find it hard to figure out what's going on, but I know what that one is."

It took several seconds for Sasa's explanation to register with Sugiko, and when it did she let out a staccato cry, "I hate it!" The card was tossed away as if it were burning hot.

After burying her face in a large pillow for a while, she lifted her head and turned her attention to a different card. There, two women lay one on top of the other, the joins of their widely spread thighs shown in close-up so that they appeared to be connected. Revealing intricate folds, their two cracks, which were pressed wide open, were a beautiful pink colour.

"What kind of people are these models?"

"Well, I guess you could say they're like prostitutes."

"I wonder if the girls in these photos are too."

"I should think so."

"And yet they're as nice a colour as this."

"Just like a virgin. They're surprisingly beautiful, aren't they? Even though they do all kinds of things," said Sasa.

"I don't like it." Sugiko's voice sounded suddenly unenthusiastic, but then it abruptly changed. "C'mon, give me a hard time!" she moaned.

On one of the cards by the pillow there was a close-up of a woman's face. It was almost regal. Three penises stuck out above her from different directions. Semen dripped from above the woman's face, wetting the side of her nose from her eye like semitransparent, white tears, and congealed white liquid collected on the lower lip of her slightly open mouth.

Sugiko's eyes were drawn toward that photograph. Seizing hold of her arms as she gazed at the picture in her aroused state, Sasa hauled her to her feet, dragging her into the room next door. He pushed her into a chair as if he were pressing her naked body into a mould. As he forced both her legs down, the backs of her knees came into contact with the chair's armrests.

"Stop it!"

Sexual emotion seeped into her weepy voice, but Sugiko's body willingly adopted its position. Wedged in the chair, with her legs splayed as wide as they would go, she couldn't move an inch. Eyes tight shut, she bent her head back in an expansive gesture; the exposed skin from a point below her chin down to her throat had turned pink and appeared to be quivering. Even having assumed that position, her thighs were only slightly apart, and the image on that card that had been discarded by the bed came to Sasa's mind. It was one of the cards she'd put in the pile of pictures she disliked and showed a close-up shot of a female's genitals, so big it seemed to fill the space on the card. It was a strange shape, the likes of which Sasa hadn't seen before and it was peculiar in its over-simplicity. There was merely one black, round open hole, and the only appendage was the clitoris. As he stared at the picture he felt strange. Unceasingly drawn into it, he thought it resembled a small, bottomless pit replete with danger.

In his mind the photograph was superimposed on Sugiko's parts. Topped by a flesh-coloured sight, the muzzle of the rifle was levelled directly at Sasa.

ONE DAY, SASA AND Sugiko ate steak at the Western restaurant. Then, standing on the road outside, they gazed at the station platform in the distance.

Sugiko lightly gripped Sasa's arm. "Let's go to the hotel," said Sasa, and she nodded quietly.

The bottle of oil he had dropped wasn't broken, and he poured a copious amount of the liquid onto the join at the top of her thighs. After a while, Sasa moved away and lay down beside her.

In a composed tone of voice Sugiko suddenly enquired, "I suppose you bleed on your wedding night, don't you?"

"I suppose so."

"I wonder if there's a way of faking it?"

"Maybe there is. You know about using Kyōbeni lipstick, right?"

"Let me see . . ."

"Kyoto geishas use it. It's made from the safflower."

"Now you mention it, I have heard of it."

"You wrap it in a fine silk cloth and insert it right to the back. Then a red colour seeps into the bed linen at just the right time."

Sasa's tone suggested he wasn't entirely serious, but Sugiko was listening intently.

"Where do they sell it?" she asked.

"At specialty lipstick stores in Kyoto."

Sugiko fell silent for a short while then spoke in a reproving voice. "Sasa-san, are you teasing me?"

"I'm sure that was one method."

"Well then, so it's true, is it?"

Sugiko wouldn't leave the subject alone.

"It's true I tell you."

"In that case I'll have to tell my friend, too."

"Your friend?"

"You don't know her. She split up with her boyfriend, and now she says she wants to pretend she's a virgin and get married. But, you know, she gets all . . ."

Sugiko faltered, her face colouring.

"What are you so embarrassed about?"

After a moment's hesitation, she continued, "She gets wet really fast, I heard."

"Even a virgin gets wet."

"But . . ."

She turned her gaze to the olive oil bottle that lay by the bed.

"It depends on the person," said Sasa, with a smile. "They say only about thirty percent of virgins bleed."

"Is that true?"

Sugiko was still gazing into space.

Seizing her shoulders and pushing her onto her back again, Sasa reached an arm out and grabbed the bottle. After a while, Sugiko suddenly spread her legs as wide as she could and shrieked, "Do something!"

For several seconds Sasa was speechless, but then an intense sexual desire welled up within him. Just as it did so, her legs abruptly came together and closed tightly. Sasa lost his head. Seized by emotions strong enough to override his fears, he tried to force himself between those thighs while Sugiko continued to let out a cry like some small animal about to be slaughtered. This time he didn't lose his erection.

From her forehead to her breast, she was shining with sweat, but, as always, it ended with Sugiko still a virgin

The emotions that had seized and incited Sasa evaporated. He disentangled himself, and Sugiko turned onto her stomach and remained motionless. Sitting up, he stared at the twin mounds below the expanse of her back. Before they had been small, like those of a girl, but now they were the buttocks of a woman. Tiny, dark brown spots stained the white sheet by her body, as if they had been sprinkled there. But she remained chaste.

No sooner had they left the hotel in Sasa's car than Sugiko had suddenly bent over in her seat.

"Aren't you feeling well?"

She shook her head. She was finding it increasingly difficult to remain emotionally detached from him. Each time they met like this, she vomited.

"Do you think you're going to throw up?"

She nodded.

The road was wide and brightly lit. Sasa made a left turn and entered a narrow street. The neighbourhood was darker than he'd expected. The steep uphill slope continued to meander, and before long it turned into a blind alley; directly ahead were the leaf scrolls of an iron gate.

Opening the door, Sasa got out of the car with Sugiko. Her back bent as she continued to vomit. Stroking her back, he left his hand there. He became aware of a faint burnt smell woven in with the night air.

Withdrawing his hand and standing on tiptoe, he surveyed the surrounding area. The scenery, which had not been visible to him, now came clearly into view. He had thought there was a large building beyond the iron gates, and through a gap in the gate he could see several black columns. A bar was suspended horizontally between each of them. Following the line of the columns, he could make out the outline of a house. It looked like the roofless remains of a residence gutted by fire.

Only the framework of the building remained, black, as if it were wet.

Supporting Sugiko's crouching body in his arms, he stroked her back.

"I feel better now."

There were tearstains in the corners of her eyes, probably from the distress of vomiting.

When they returned to the car, she asked quietly, "What will become of us?"

"I don't know," he replied, starting the engine.

"Drive me home tonight, please," she said.

It was about an hour and a half journey by car to her neighbourhood, and it seemed a bother to Sasa to have to do it that night.

The smell of the fire lingered faintly in the car. He wondered why that should be. Had the odour they had freely breathed in several minutes ago tainted their lungs? Surely that wasn't possible.

He casually tried bringing his face close to Sugiko's hair, and the smell became a shade stronger. It clung to her hair.

"Can't you smell something?" asked Sasa.

Inhaling a long, slow breath, Sugiko said, "Yes, you're right. Something like rain—or smoke." She brought her nose close to his shoulder. "Your suit smells of it."

Maybe the smell had secreted itself into the fibres too. *Something like rain or smoke, was it*? Such a lyrical expression wasn't apt.

"Is it my suit? Maybe I should put it in for cleaning."

Sugiko couldn't have seen the house while she'd been crouching down before.

"But it's not a bad smell. It seems something a bit sad," she said.

Sasa opened the car window a little, but he sensed the smell would linger faintly forever.

Chapter 3   Scratches

On Sunday afternoon, Sasa had a phone call from Yūko.

"Sugiko's round at my place. Won't you come over?" she asked.

He'd seen Sugiko just the day before. He found it all tiresome, much in the same way he wouldn't have wanted to think about alcohol had he been suffering from a hangover. Feeling his age the way he did at times like this, Sasa replied, "I don't know whereabouts you live."

"I told you just the other day, didn't I?"

"I don't remember."

"I'll tell you again. Sugiko says she wants to talk to you about something."

"I'm actually a little busy right now."

"She says she's arranged to go to a friend's house tonight, and I think she'd be happy if you came over just for a little while."

Deciding he'd better go, Sasa got himself ready. As he left the room, his wife called to him, "Oh, are you going out?"

"There's some business I have to attend to. I'll be back before dark," he replied simply, and stepped outside.

The rain had started in the afternoon. He drove toward the city for about thirty minutes, then got out on a road lined with rows of trees. It was late autumn and the trees were bare. Following the directions he'd been given, he turned a corner and went into an alleyway. The third building he came across was a small, Western-style house. Beyond the front door a short, narrow corridor extended towards the back of the house.

There was a guest room at the rear and a small room on the right side of the corridor. From the open door he could see a single bed. Sugiko was sitting in a chair in the guest's room.

Pulling a gas heater close and crouching over it, she turned her head toward Sasa. "I got soaked on the way here."

Sitting down in a chair nearby, he turned to Yūko. "You have a nice place, but the layout's a little strange. The living room and guest room are the wrong way round, aren't they? And there's a bed right next to the entrance hall."

"If I put the bed in here it'd be too cramped."

Yūko used her eyes to indicate a large, rectangular table in the corner of the room. He had heard she worked as a designer in a dressmaker's, but didn't know the details.

"Do you work at home too, using that table?"

"Yes. I've just taken Sugiko's measurements."

Sugiko was Yūko's customer as well as her friend.

"You must know her measurements pretty well."

"I do, but she says her body has changed recently. She sure was right!"

Yūko gave Sasa a sidelong glance, the corners of her eyes seeming to smile at him.

"I told you so the other day, didn't I? I noticed it this summer," said Sugiko.

"That's right. You said you couldn't get into your swimsuits anymore, or something."

A look of embarrassment passed across Sugiko's face, and he thought there was a hint of self-contempt in it.

"Yūko said you wanted to see me about something. What is it?"

Sugiko's face flushed a light, pale red and she looked angry.

"It's nothing. Do we need a reason to see each other? Or are you saying *that* is the reason we meet up?"

Just then the phone rang in the bedroom. Yūko got up and left the room.

— 155 —

Gazing again at Sugiko, Sasa noticed she was barefoot. "Say, you've nothing on your feet."

"I got wet, so I'm drying my stockings."

There were some slippers by the chair where she'd kicked them off.

Sasa stared at her feet. Though he'd seen her naked any number of times, it was the first time he'd noticed the shape of her feet. Why, he wondered, had his eyes not been drawn toward them before now? Her toes were long and slender, and only the area around the joints jutted out. Leaning forward, he held her toes between his fingers, about where the joints were.

"It's the first time I've looked at them."

Still leaning forward, he turned his head and gazed up at her.

"My feet are unsightly, don't you think?" said Sugiko, panting. Aroused, her face was suffused with blood.

Sasa was excited too. "They're exactly the same shape as mine. Even so, I wonder why I haven't noticed them until now."

Letting go, he stood up, and, threading his arms under her armpits, he lifted her out of the chair. Rising from her seat, she stood up and faced him. Their bodies came together, and through the material of their clothes their bellies touched. They could still hear Yūko's voice on the phone in the bedroom. It was a long call. Sasa slipped his arm around Sugiko's back and pulled the zipper down.

"I'm going to strip you naked," he whispered in her ear.

Gripping both Sasa's arms so hard the tips of her fingernails dug into his flesh, Sugiko said, in a husky voice, "Do it!"

He wondered what Yūko would say if she came back in and found every stitch of Sugiko's clothing had been removed.

They heard the faint click of the phone as Yūko hung up.

"We'd better give it up for today."

As he moved away from Sugiko, having done her zipper slowly back up, Yūko came in. There was a strained atmosphere suggesting something had happened, and even Sasa himself was conscious of it.

"What's the matter? You're both standing up." She looked from one to the other and said, in a frank tone of voice, "Sugiko, your face is red."

"She's excited, that's why," cut in Sasa, with equal candour.

"Oh. You can use my bed if you like," said Yūko, with no sign of abashment.

Sasa moved around behind Sugiko's chair, where she was now sitting, and placed both hands on her shoulders. She seemed to be about to get up, and so, applying some pressure, he held her in the chair and then said to Yūko, "You're ingrained in that bed. If we use it, the three of us will end up in it together."

"That's an erotic way of putting it, isn't it?"

"As I said, we'd better leave it."

"How come?"

"You'll end up getting caught up in this too."

"*Getting caught up in it . . .* You mean the three of us ending up in bed together? That's alright, isn't it?"

Moving his hands away from Sugiko's shoulders, Sasa looked again at Yūko.

"What's your relationship with Sugiko?"

"You first, Sasa-san."

"You already know from Sugiko, don't you?"

"I heard she was still a virgin. Is that true?"

Sasa had become acquainted with every inch of Sugiko's body, and it was only intercourse that she had not permitted. Whenever he looked at her obstinately shrinking form, he lost his erection.

"I guess that's right. Her warranty is still in effect."

"Why do you leave the situation so ambiguous? Get on with it, and void the warranty!"

"Don't think I haven't thought about it."

"You're afraid. You can't force yourself on her."

"I tried to do that," said Sasa, with a wry smile.

"In that case the timing is just right. Please, go ahead and use my bed."

"Why is it just right?"

A vague smile surfaced on Yūko's face.

Sugiko had remained seated while they were talking; she was obviously tense.

"That's a shame. I don't feel up to it today."

As if to bring the conversation with Yūko to a close, Sasa said to Sugiko, "You're going to your friend's house, aren't you? What time do you have to be there?"

"They'll probably already have got together."

"In that case, you'd better hurry up and go."

"It's OK to get there late. We just get together for no particular reason, you see."

"You'd better get going. What about you, Yūko?"

"I'm not going. I'd be out of place amongst a bunch of young kids," said Yūko, who was just a shade older than Sugiko.

"I can drive by your friend's house on my way home. How about I drop you there?"

Sugiko replied in a harsh voice. "Sasa-san, you're trying to force me on that bunch of young guys, aren't you?"

"You're wrong. I'm trying to return you to them is all."

Urging Sugiko along, he stood up and went outside. It was still raining, and, opening an umbrella, he drew her under it. Exiting the alleyway, he noticed a liquor store on the opposite side of the tree-lined road. "To say sorry for making you late, let me buy some whisky. You could take it with you," said Sasa.

"I don't need anything like that," replied Sugiko, shrugging him off and walking briskly away. She left the shelter of the umbrella, and the raindrops appeared pale as they rained down on her.

On the evening of December 24, Sugiko called. She said she was drinking with Yūko and the others and asked whether he could come. She told him the name of the bar in the back streets of the downtown area. Sasa knew it; it was a small, dingy drinking hole.

Sasa hesitated, and Sugiko said, "Are you celebrating Christmas Eve at home?"

"We don't do anything like that."

"In that case, why don't you come out?"

Sasa agreed and put the phone down.

As he was getting ready, his wife came into the room, and said, "Are you going out? Can't you spend time with Naoko just for once? It's Christmas Eve, after all."

"Naoko—is she in second grade or third?"

"That was unkind. You know very well she's in second grade. And to think, she's your own daughter! But why are you going out?"

"Why?" parroted Sasa, as he thought about it. *Why am I going out?* he wondered.

Even after they'd gone their separate ways in that awkward manner a month or so ago, he'd continued to see Sugiko. Whenever they met they would go to a hotel together. It was as if Sasa felt there was no other point to their meeting. But it didn't look as though he would be able to be alone with her tonight.

"Yes, I wonder why," he muttered, adding, "I'll be right back."

He decided to go by car. He didn't feel like drinking this evening. He would pay the bar bill and then return home. Occasionally it was good to do what a middle-aged man was supposed to do.

But why? Was he taking the trouble to go out just for that? Sasa mulled this over as he drove.

He opened the bar door and saw the backs of customers lined up in a row, drinking at the counter.

Sugiko and Yūko were on the left, one on either side of a young man, and there were glasses of alcohol on the table. Noticing Sasa, Sugiko tilted her head a little to one side and smiled. Sasa liked that gesture. Did liking subtle gestures—the way she moved her shoulder, the shape of her lips when she opened her mouth, or the way she bent her arm—mean he liked all of her? Had he really come all the way out here to see that?

The three were sitting a little apart. Settling himself down next to Sugiko, Sasa looked around the bar; the cramped interior was full. There were customers of various ages, but he clearly looked out of place sitting with Sugiko and her friends. Yet only Yūko knew about his relationship with her. He had mixed feelings as he contemplated this, and he took out a cigarette and lit it.

"Would you like a drink?" asked Sugiko.

Sugiko could hold her liquor and her face hadn't changed colour. He couldn't tell how much she'd had to drink, even now.

"Yeah, why not? I'll just have one."

"Why just one?"

"I brought the car, you see. I'm planning on going home soon."

"Aren't you having a good time, hanging out with everyone like this?"

"I can't really tonight."

Sugiko fell silent.

Sasa went to the toilet. As he opened the door to go back out, he could see Sugiko and her friends. From where he was standing those were the only seats visible.

Sugiko was there, her arms wound around the young guy's neck, face tilted up, her lips pressed against his. He could tell she had her tongue down his throat. Having briefly come to a halt, Sasa returned unconcernedly to his seat, only this time he sat next to Yūko. Everyone in the bar was watching the young couple.

The young man seemed to be pretty drunk, and, unable to deal with the intense scrutiny they had attracted, tried to pull away from Sugiko. Sugiko hooked her arms around him even more firmly, running her fingers through his hair. She kissed him expertly, her arms snaking sinuously around his neck with sensual movements.

Even once they'd separated, she muttered something with a nasal twang and immediately sought his lips again. Jeering voices began to reverberate around the hitherto quiet bar.

"Let's see you go all the way!"

Sasa was sitting uncomfortably next to Yūko. He thought he ought to shout a quick-witted word or two, but he felt powerless in the face of the dexterity and intensity of the kiss.

"She still seems inexperienced. The movements of her fingertips aren't delicate enough," he ventured, but the way she used her fingers was nearly perfect. Sasa was afraid that Yūko's questioning gaze would turn in his direction. He wasn't sure he could look as unconcerned as he wanted to.

"I wonder if Sugiko really is a virgin," whispered Yūko.

Perhaps Yūko had guessed how Sasa felt, but at the same time that was what she really wanted to know. Certainly the way Sugiko was carrying on right now had aroused her curiosity.

"When it comes right down to it, I guess only she knows the answer to that."

"I bet you know, Sasa-san."

"More or less, I suppose," he replied, regaining his composure.

Once the feeling of being caught off-guard had subsided, the image of Sugiko, who would allow anything but *that* when they were together in private, superimposed itself on the figure of Sugiko in front of him.

"Still, she's good at it, don't you think?" said Yūko.

The kiss was still continuing.

YŪKO WATCHED SUGIKO AND the young man move apart, and then said, "We'd better get going or we'll be late."

"Where to?"

Yūko mentioned the name of a street about thirty minutes' drive away.

"There's a party there."

"A bunch of young kids?"

"That's right."

"I thought you said before you weren't going to a get-together like that."

"It's Christmas Eve, so we decided to hang out with them."

"So why did you have me come out here?"

"It was Sugiko's idea to call you."

Sugiko and the young man had gotten up.

Sasa settled the bill, and when he went outside he found the three of them standing right in front of him.

"I'll drive you and then go home from there," said Sasa, seizing Sugiko by the arm. The car would have accommodated the four of them, but he'd made it clear that he wasn't in the mood. Sugiko was pulled along in silence. He put her in the front passenger seat and started the car. She remained quiet.

After a little while, Sasa said, "Are you doing it with that guy just now?"

"We're not especially close."

"You could have fooled me!"

"You told me yourself that I'd better go back to the young set, didn't you?"

He drove on without replying. Sasa knew there was only one love hotel in the neighborhood they were headed to. The hotel was on the second floor of a tired-looking building, and there was just a bed in each small, rectangular room. In order to bathe, you had to wait for the only bathroom on that floor to become free. The building was right behind the downtown area, and the neighbourhood was dismal.

He stopped the car next to the hotel.

"It's further on," said Sugiko.

"We're getting out here."

The hotel sign, in the shape of a lantern hanging from the eaves, was lit up in front of Sugiko, who'd gotten out of the car.

"We can't do this. Those two will be worried."

"It won't take long."

Giving her shoulder a shove, he pushed her into the building. Sugiko resisted slightly but moved as he pushed her.

Taking the key from the front desk clerk, they climbed the stairs. The gloomy, narrow corridor stretched ahead of them. Near the end of the corridor was a room that matched the number on the key. There was a dry sound as the lock turned. As they entered, the bedsheets stood out in white relief in the midst of the dim room.

No matter what Sugiko wore, Sasa knew precisely the location of the hooks and buttons. He stripped her naked, standing where they were in the middle of the floor. He was going to leave her shoes and stockings on but then reconsidered and removed them. He flung the balled-up stockings as hard as he could into a corner of the room. Gripping Sugiko's arms as she began to shrink away, Sasa pulled her back up and then pushed her away. She collapsed face down on the bed.

She had a lustrous, white body, a sack of skin brimming with youthfulness. The line from her abdomen to the bulge of her hips was somewhat immature. He moved to the bed and used both hands to partially turn her. The strength left her upturned body and her limbs were splayed. Sasa gazed at her silent form and then looked at his watch. Only five minutes had elapsed since they'd entered the room.

"It's getting late. Put your clothes on."

Sugiko turned her head and looked at him and then got off the bed. Wearily she pulled her clothes on.

When he paid the bill, having returned the key, the middle-aged front desk clerk gave them a suspicious look, as though she were thinking, *My, my. An older man and a young woman going into a room and coming out again not ten minutes later.*

Doubtless she would never guess what had really gone on during that time.

Sugiko remained quiet even after they'd gotten into the car. Starting the engine, Sasa asked, "Where's the place?"

"Eh?"

"The place where the party is."

"Oh, yes, drive straight on."

For a while all he heard was her voice issuing directions.

"Turn right."

"Turn left at that corner."

"I think it's at the end of that street."

The road came to a dead-end and then turned off to the right. Two people stood on the corner.

"Ah, it's Yūko," said Sugiko, and Sasa stopped the car. Remaining in his seat, he reached over, opened the passenger door and let her out.

The heater was on, so the windows were closed. Lowering the driver's side window, he called out, "Why are you standing out here?"

Yūko, who'd approached the open window, replied, "Because you're pretty late, and we were worried about you."

"How long have you been waiting?"

"About fifteen minutes, I guess."

"We took the wrong road."

Sugiko, who'd just gotten out of the car, stood close by Yūko.

"What were you worried about?"

"We thought you'd had an accident or something."

"An accident?" murmured Sasa, looking at Sugiko.

He was aware that a faint smile had surfaced on his face. Sugiko drew near the still-open window of the car. In the next instant, one hand, with its fingertips curled into five hooks, shot through the air, and Sasa was left with a stinging coldness on his right cheek. He stared wordlessly at Sugiko as a stiff smile appeared on her face.

Facing forward, without changing his expression, he slowly started the car.

Turning right at the corner, he drove the car out onto the wide road and took off. After a while he began to feel pain. He ran his left hand over his cheek, and his fingertips came away wet with blood. Once again, he probed around with his fingertips and tried touching the wound: there were three long, thin gashes running in parallel on the surface of his cheek. Recovering his senses, he realised the car was crossing a bridge which spanned a wide river. The road stretched on into the distance, in the opposite direction to his house.

Chapter 4   The Policeman in the Night

As Sasa drove along the expressway that night, an area bordered by yellow lights—fairly wide and elliptical in shape—came into view directly ahead.

He knew the sea was that way and wondered if it was the harbour. He could see several small freighters at anchor, a lamp burning from each of their two masts. The road swept to the right, and the car ran straight along the coast. Whenever he saw the ocean he always felt a sort of excitement as he breathed the sea air in deeply. It didn't seem to be merely because he lived in the city with little or no opportunity to see the ocean, either. He wasn't sure himself why he reacted that way.

He repeatedly turned his head in the direction of the ocean and then quickly back again; the black surface of the sea was running a little high. A forest of chimneys lined the coast. Red lights glowed from several of them. A myriad of yellow lights shone here and there, faintly illuminating the small wave crests forming on the surface of the sea. A tall, narrow tower came into view, and close to the top a single orange light shone out.

As he repeatedly looked out to sea and back again, he felt as if a fissure would appear at any moment in the expressway as it stretched on into the distance, flanked on either side by lights. At those moments he caught brief glimpses of water through chinks in the curtain of bright light.

The behaviour Sugiko exhibited in private appeared in each flashing glimpse of water. He could see her various attitudes in the water's somewhat troubled surface: Sugiko's compliant self, Sugiko shrinking away from him, Sugiko rejecting him.

That Sugiko was now sitting in the seat next to him. Sasa had come out of the hotel room with her a little while before.

"What are you looking at?" she asked, noticing his behaviour.

"The sea."

With her forehead pressed against the window, she gazed a while at the scenery outside.

"Is that really the sea? It's just dirty, black water, isn't it?"

"So dirty and black that you can't marry anyone, you mean? You needn't worry. You're still a virgin," said Sasa.

This pattern in their relationship had been going on for nearly a year and a half.

"But why do you care?"

"Because I want to get married in a pure white dress."

Sugiko spoke the words she always repeated like some kind of incantation.

"If that's what you want, there's no reason to spend time with the likes of me. You can wear a white wedding dress whenever you want, can't you?"

"Sasa-san, can't you marry me?" she said.

Over forty and with a wife and child, he said nothing.

"Anyhow, I think it's high time you stopped yelling 'Ow!' and 'Stop it!' and things like that when we're in the hotel," said Sasa after a while.

"If I stop, it's you that will suffer, Sasa-san."

"You know, for all that you are very good at it," he said, reaching out and lightly brushing her lip with the tip of his middle finger.

With a sigh, she wrapped her lips around his finger and gradually took it deeply into her mouth. She ran the tip of her tongue teasingly over the joints of his finger, and, when before long he pulled it out of her mouth, she applied her tongue to the base of the gap between his ring finger and little finger, all the while using her tongue skilfully.

Just as her tongue made its way slowly up the inside of his little finger as far as the tip, Sugiko suddenly lay face down in his lap and remained there motionless. Her ragged breathing continued, and he felt her hot breath through his trousers.

A SIGNBOARD CAME INTO view indicating the exit from the expressway. Sasa moved the hand he'd been resting on the nape of Sugiko's neck and pulled her face away. Tonight was the first time she'd done anything like that in the car.

He manoeuvred the car over to the right to leave the expressway. He drove down the exit ramp, and, coming out on the road at the bottom, he turned right and came to the end of a wide road where there was a set of traffic lights. While they were waiting at the red light, a policeman, who'd been standing in front of the police box on the corner, came over and signalled to them.

The window was lowered and the policeman brought his face in close, "Have you been drinking?"

"No, officer."

"Let me see your driver's licence."

Sasa put his hand in the back pocket of his trousers, but it was empty. He realised he'd changed his suit earlier and neglected to transfer his driver's licence.

"Ah, I've forgotten it. I changed my clothes earlier, you see."

"Please step out of the car."

He and Sugiko went inside the police box.

"Failing to carry a driver's licence, eh?" said the policeman.

Sasa looked at him a little disconcertedly.

The officer was perhaps slightly older than he was, smallish and with prominent cheekbones. Sasa lost no time in reading his character. Failing to carry a driver's licence wasn't an especially serious crime, but it might take time to sort out depending on how things progressed.

"If you forgot it while you were changing your clothes, it would be in your house then, wouldn't it?" said the policeman.

"Er, . . ." replied Sasa, vaguely.

There was no doubt it was in his house, but . . .

"Can't you telephone home and have someone bring it here?"

"No one's home."

"No one's home? At your house?"

"I left it at my office."

Reflexively, Sasa blurted out an inspired lie; he couldn't very well do as the policeman had asked.

The middle-aged policeman quietly looked from Sasa to Sugiko. He seemed like the kind of guy who would enjoy an evening drink with his family. Sasa and Sugiko looked to him neither like father and daughter nor elder brother and sister.

Sasa's mind was working feverishly to find a way out of this predicament unscathed. He had to admit he'd lost his composure. Since his youth, he'd always found himself in situations like this in his dealings with girls. He had always chosen to walk on the shady side, avoiding people's gazes. It had been that way even in his relationship with the woman he married.

He looked at his watch. It showed 11:00 p.m. It would take another hour to reach Sugiko's neighbourhood, and it would be half past midnight by the time the last train arrived at the station close to her home. She would have to make out she'd caught that train if she were to smooth things over with her parents, and time was gradually running out.

Sasa felt he had to say something, and, at length, he thought of something to placate the policeman. "I'd like to get this young lady back to her home quickly. How about I do this: I'll drop by my office on the way back, collect my driver's licence and come back here with it?"

Even assuming the policeman allowed him to go, it would be pretty difficult to return home briefly and then come right out again in the middle of the night. But it would be all the more troublesome if Sugiko didn't make the last train home.

"Hmm." The policeman was looking from one to the other as before. "What's your name? I can make inquiries, and if I find the driver's licence is issued in that name then I'll overlook what happened tonight."

Relieved, Sasa gave him his name.

"And your date of birth?" added the policeman.

Sasa replied, and, looking from Sugiko to Sasa once more, the policeman walked quietly over to the telephone. It was likely to take a while to get an answer. As Sasa imagined the awkward silence while they waited, Sugiko extended her right palm in front of him and said in a low voice, "See, my nails are nice, aren't they?"

The fingers of her right hand were pressed together, with no gaps between them, and held out in front of his eyes.

Those fingers, with their inconspicuous joints, were slender and pliant, though the shape of the nails—manicured and coated with transparent polish—was nothing to be especially proud of. He was about to take no notice, but then suddenly something caught his eye. They weren't long nails at all, and while they ought to have been a uniform length and well-shaped, the nails he saw before him looked short.

"So they are," said Sasa, deliberately, staring at her right hand.

Her fingernails had been pared to the quick. Taking hold of her left hand and scrutinising her fingers, he found that all its nails had been clipped short. Suddenly, in his mind's eye the image of a man began to cover Sugiko's body. The dark image, with its obscure outline, slowly grew bigger.

"I guess you scratched someone, didn't you? Because he held you down and cut your nails. I bet it was just your index finger, am I right?" Quietly, he said what had occurred to him.

"Just my index finger."

"You trimmed the others neatly yourself, didn't you?"

"Why! You've found me out, haven't you?"

— 170 —

As she spoke, there was something in her expression that suggested she was dropping a hint. In that moment she looked grave, although neither her expression nor her reply indicated Sasa had guessed correctly.

Why, he wondered, *had she behaved that way*?

"Just recently you went for a drive with someone, didn't you?"

"How perceptive of you," she said, her voice a quiet murmur.

At that time it probably hadn't been fingers that she'd had in her mouth either. A picture of Sugiko as she went down between the thighs of the man in the driver's seat came to Sasa unbidden. The man would pull the car over to the shoulder and stop. After that, Sugiko's nails would fly through the air. *But where had the nail clippers been?* he wondered. Had they been in Sugiko's handbag all along? Perhaps they had been used in the hotel room.

"Aren't you jealous?" she said.

He looked at her and noticed a defiant gleam in her eye. But the sort of jealousy that would clearly rankle didn't well up inside him. For the first time, Sasa realised the existence of another man wouldn't present an obstacle to him. The question that had tumbled so easily from her mouth bothered him far more than that.

Sasa had spoken to the policeman using language that deliberately obscured their relationship. As he watched the policeman, with the receiver glued to his ear, the policeman's lips twitched. The results of the enquiry were doubtless being relayed to him through the earpiece. Before long he replaced the receiver and turned to face Sasa.

"It's been confirmed a driver's licence was issued to you." Sasa waited quietly for him to continue. "You are free to go. I will overlook it just this once."

The policeman drew close to Sugiko and said, "Take care going home."

He didn't glance in Sasa's direction, and although his voice was benign, the underlying meaning was clear.

"Yes, thank you."

Sasa stared at Sugiko's lips as she spoke. There was still something lingering within her that he would have to watch out for, but it was something beyond the policeman's imagination.

"You were very helpful, thank you."

Sasa thanked the policeman, still staring openly at Sugiko's lips. Conscious of his gaze, she opened and closed her mouth slightly, and for a moment he could see the tongue inside. Leaving the police box, they walked over to the car, and, still gazing at those lips, he opened the door.

Chapter 5   Blood

THE COAST ROAD LOOPED round in a gentle curve and then began to climb uphill. Running her eyes over the clock on the dashboard in front of Sasa, whose hands were on the steering wheel, Sugiko said, "Another thirty minutes. We'll make it in plenty of time."

Her hometown was beyond the low mountain range they were about to traverse. It was midnight. The road carved into the hillside was dark, and few cars passed that way. Only the dashboard indicators and the clock in front of them were round and bright in the darkness.

"Cars do break down, you know. It would have been better to go home by train," said Sasa.

"It's tedious being alone. Besides, you've a duty to see me home, Sasa-san."

"A duty? Ha!"

Sasa laid his hand on Sugiko's thigh as she sat beside him. Her flesh went rigid for a moment but soon softened.

"Say, do you think we can say we're courting?" she asked, abruptly.

"No one uses old-fashioned phrases like that anymore, do they?"

"I hear it a lot."

"You do? So?"

"So, what does it mean?"

"You know, don't you?"

"In that case, what does that make us?"

"How shall I put it? In short, it means we're in an illicit relationship."

"That's a horrible way of describing it. Anyway, are we courting, or aren't we?"

"You can't put it like that. Fact is, we're in a casual relationship, and that's all there is to it."

The macadam road petered out, and the car began to rumble. Sugiko was quiet. Ahead, the mouth of a tunnel loomed into view.

"Have we been seeing each other for a year and a half already?" she said.

"Will be soon, I guess."

"A year and a half. That's a heck of a long time." Sugiko's voice suddenly brightened, her cheerfulness making Sasa feel uneasy. "I've learned a lot, so, I don't mind if I die now."

"There's no need for that kind of talk. You're still only . . ."

He broke off. It seemed to him more trouble than it was worth to say it.

The road had become terribly uneven, and he gripped the steering wheel forcefully. The car entered the tunnel through the mountain. The road inside was long and straight. Before long, the exit came indistinctly into view.

Ahead, two parallel lines of small red lights studded the road surface into the near distance. They gave off little light as their red glow seeped into the dark night.

By the light of a sign indicating that construction work was in progress, they could see one side of the road had been dug up for quite a stretch.

"It looks like a will-o'-the wisp, doesn't it?"

"Yes, they must be lit up for a fairy's wedding procession," said Sugiko. "It's pitch black—nothing out there other than those red lights."

As the car sped along, she peered around and gave a small cry, "Oh!"

"What's the matter?"

"Look behind you, quickly now." Her voice was playful. "Quickly, quickly."

Bobbing up and down in her seat, she urged him to take a look. She was acting like a frolicsome child, and Sasa found her behaviour odd. The car was still in the tunnel. Slowing down, he turned and looked over his shoulder with a sweeping movement. He couldn't see anything. There wasn't so much as a faint light, only a wall of darkness, like a board painted black as ink. Sugiko's laughter sounded shrill and cheerful in his ear.

HALF OF THE NARROW road had been dug up. As they passed that area, the road began to slope gently downhill, and scores of lights from the town came into view. Sasa pulled onto the hard shoulder of the road, which had become wider, and brought the car to a halt, still gripping the steering wheel as he rested his forehead on the backs of his hands. "I'm beat," he sighed, adding, "That tunnel's finished me off."

"It was very dark, wasn't it?" If anything, Sugiko's tone this time was melancholy.

"It was pitch black in there, like a film covering my eyes."

When Sasa was dog-tired, he sometimes felt agitated, as if his nerve endings were burning. Reaching out, he grabbed Sugiko around the neck and pulled her in close. Whenever this happened these days she immediately went down on him. There would be the rough sound of the zipper being pulled down, and Sugiko's lips would part. Applying gentle pressure with those moist lips, she would move her head up and down as she manipulated her tongue, almost too adroitly at times. And when he came, she would close her eyes and gulp it down, and the smell of semen would linger a while in her mouth and on her lips. But this time, she resisted Sasa's forceful advances.

"What's the matter?"

"My house is close by."

"Even so," he began, but then he realised what she was trying to say. She was afraid of going into her parents' house with that pungent smell clinging to her lips.

The lights inside her home were warm and inviting, and the outline of her family, whom Sasa had never met, was filled in with black. Sugiko would go into the house wearing an air of innocence, her lips clamped tightly shut to prevent that odour rising up from her stomach.

Sasa was wildly excited as he imagined that scene. He applied still more pressure and tried to draw her to him, but Sugiko dug her nails into the back of his hand. They froze as they were, their eyes drawn to the back of his hand and her sharp nails.

"You feel like wounding me again?" he asked. "If you really don't want to do it, then why not go ahead and scratch me?"

After a moment's hesitation, her nails moved slowly on the surface of Sasa's skin, the forceful motion seemingly revealing a pent-up hatred. Sasa held his hand up and stared at the back of it as blood coursed from the two long gashes.

"Sorry, but I don't want to," she said, turning toward the window.

With his hand still dripping blood, Sasa turned the engine over and started the car. They sat in silence as they descended the slope and approached the multitude of lights. They went over a railroad crossing and, letting Sugiko off near the station building, he said, "See you again," before making a U-turn and driving away.

He went back the way he'd come. Passing by the red lights, he entered the tunnel, the car's headlights throwing light on the blackness of the interior. A cavity formed in a recess of his mind, in the midst of which something vague and formless stirred incessantly.

The car ran along at a moderate speed. At the foot of the mountain pass the road suddenly broadened out. Sasa approached a fork in the road. Straight on and he would come out at the coast road, while the other road curved gently to the left. As he continued down the road ahead, he felt a slight impact, as if someone had brought their hands down lightly on the rear of the car's body. Looking back, a motorcycle, with a man sitting astride it, was slowly toppling over to the right of the car. For a moment Sasa was taken aback. Coming from the right, as he was going straight on, the motorcycle had collided with the car as it tried to turn into the road on the left, the rider probably assuming Sasa too was turning left. But now wasn't the time to question which driver was at fault.

This was going to be trouble, and, seized by an intense feeling of unease, Sasa stopped the car and got out. There was no traffic at all on the road. The man, who'd fallen over at an angle while still holding the handlebars, had stood up, together with the motorcycle.

"What happened?"

The man was silent. He'd fallen off in the middle of an intersection.

"Let's go over the other side. Can you walk?"

He pushed his motorcycle along, and Sasa went with him over near the street corner. Toppling the brand new motorcycle over onto the sidewalk, the man crouched down. He was young, and his feet were slipped into a pair of flip-flops.

Sasa looked frantically about. On the corner opposite he noticed a house with a light on. From its appearance he could tell it was a liquor store, and he briefly wondered why it was still open in the middle of the night. In any case, he concluded that they were bound to have a phone.

"Are you injured?" he said, looking at the man. There was no blood evident, but he was concerned about the possibility of internal bleeding. "Shall I call an ambulance?"

"No, there's no need for that," replied the man, rolling out of his squatting posture and lying down on the ground on his back. He had one hand placed against his forehead.

"There'll be a phone in that liquor store over there. I should call all the same."

All sorts of things were going to come to light, Sasa thought. He'd better think up a plausible story. But . . .

"Leave it, will you. I'm fine. If I just lie here for a while, I'll be OK in no time," the other protested weakly.

Suddenly, Sasa said something that surprised even him. "Shall I go and buy a bottle of lemonade?"

It was winter, hardly the season for cold drinks.

"No. Cola would be good though," replied the man, pressing a hand against his face, covering his forehead as before.

"Are you sure? Anyhow, if you're going to lie down you'd be better off in the car."

Opening the rear door of the car, he placed his hand on the man, who crawled into the back and lay down facing upwards.

He wasn't able to get the man's legs completely in, so he left the door open. Sasa walked over to the liquor store and went inside. A plump, middle-aged woman was sitting in back, and, even though she'd seen him, she said nothing. Looking over his shoulder, he could see his car directly out front and the motorcycle lying on its side on the ground. The man's legs, from the knees down were sticking out the car door, but the woman didn't say anything. The look on her face suggested the scene in front of her didn't exist. Sasa ascertained there was a telephone nearby. It would have been preferable to sort all this out without having to use the phone, he thought.

He said to the woman, "I'll take a cola, please."

"Eh? A cola, you say?"

Her face softened. She'd probably been afraid of becoming involved in the matter. He took the opened cola and swigged it from the bottle, downing it in three gulps. He realised for the first time he'd been thirsty.

"Open another one, would you please?" He put his money on the counter and she handed him the bottle.

"You don't need to return it," she said.

When he came out of the liquor store, the young man had gotten out of the car and was standing up. Sasa handed him the bottle. He took it with a nod, put the bottle to his lips and tipped his head back. Drinking only half of it, he set the bottle down on the kerb and raised his motorcycle up.

"Your bike isn't scratched, is it?" said Sasa.

"No, not at all," answered the man, though the handlebars were slightly bent. He jumped on the kick start lever. There was a dull noise as the engine tried to catch, but it soon stopped. He tried once again, but the result was the same.

Just then, Sasa realised something. He hadn't once made eye contact with the young man; he'd been trying to avoid catching Sasa's eye.

I get it. Maybe this guy has a predicament of his own. Maybe that's why he didn't want me to call an ambulance, he thought. Even so, assuming his engine wouldn't start, Sasa would have to load the motorcycle into the car and take him to wherever he was going. Just as he started worrying anew that the bike wouldn't fit in the car, he heard the powerful reverberation of the engine.

"Well, that's that."

Still without catching Sasa's eye, the man straddled the motorcycle and sped off.

ONE EVENING, A FEW days later, Sasa found himself alone in one of his regular bars. While he was sitting drinking in one of the booths, Sonoko came over and sat down next to him. Before long, she noticed his wound – two still-raw, blood-stained gashes side by side on the back of his hand.

"Oh, that tells its own story. Did you have a row with your wife?"

"No."

"Was it a cat?"

"I don't have a cat."

"I see. Something juicier then?"

Transfixed by the blood, her eyes were shining, evidently excited by the sight of his wound. Sasa had heard she was the sort of woman who didn't get excited unless she was slapped around a little. He wondered if her eyes were so bright because she felt as if it was she that had been scratched. Then again maybe he was reading too much into it. He didn't even know if the rumours were true.

Occasionally, he would have dinner with Sonoko after the bar closed, but that was as far as their relationship went. There was a powerful feeling of intimacy between them, but she didn't arouse in him any strong desires. There was an attraction about Sonoko, and Sasa found there to be a pleasure in continuing this intimate, if ambiguous relationship with such a woman.

"What have you been up to lately?" she enquired, in a slightly more formal tone.

"It's . . . a little complicated."

"So it would seem."

She looked again at the back of his hand. "I wonder what time it is," she said.

"It's already pretty late. This is the third place I've dropped by for a drink."

Sonoko was sitting on Sasa's right. She reached out, pulled his left cuff up a little and looked at his watch. The sleeve of her kimono lightly brushed his cheek and the fragrance of her perfume was heavy.

"We're closing soon," she said, letting her fingertips stroke the surface of his wound; in that instant, the back of his hand trembled.

"Does it still bother you?"

"A little."

"What have you been doing?" she said, with a suppressed laugh. "Let's go somewhere for another drink. You can tell me all about it."

Sasa thought it was good to talk with Sonoko, and he felt he might be able to reappraise his relationship with Sugiko. At the same time, he also wanted to deepen the complex ambiguity of their relationship by discussing some of the explicit details.

THEY ATE A LIGHT meal at a late-night restaurant near Sonoko's apartment. When she asked what had happened from the other side of the table, Sasa realised his urge to discuss the details of his relationship with Sugiko had evaporated.

"Never mind. It's too much trouble."

"Yet you were willing to discuss it before."

"You seemed excited about it, that's why."

"So, you wanted to get me more excited. Is that it?"

"Well, maybe. It's not something that can be pigeonholed so neatly, especially by a man my age."

"If you put it that way, maybe you're right," she answered. She levelled her gaze at the back of Sasa's left hand, and added, "But I don't mind if you just give me the highlights."

Sasa told her about it briefly. It took perhaps three or four minutes.

"That is really horrid," she said, as if to herself.

"I'm glad you agree. Don't you think it's a little too manipulative, just protecting her virginity and having a half-baked relationship? Although I am quite interested in her manipulative side."

"Oh, I was referring to you, Sasa."

He faltered. "But why?"

"To a girl of that age, the man she's dating seems like the best thing in the world. And so she'll end up doing anything for him."

"Not necessarily *anything*."

"But you have her do all kinds of things, don't you?"

"She wants to do them."

"Still it's you, Sasa, that makes her do them."

Holding the liquid from the glass in his mouth, he fell silent for a while.

"I never imagined you had a fondness for virgins."

"That's not necessarily true, but if they happen to be, . . ." he continued, somewhat defensively. Since it was Sonoko he was talking to he felt inclined to discuss it. "You know, you've misunderstood me. It's not that I'm interested in purity or anything like that. There's something very special in the way a virgin responds. That's what interests me."

"If that's the case, you really are bad."

"Trying to see it from a woman's point of view, I have my doubts about people these days making out it doesn't mean anything to be a virgin. I personally know a woman who said she felt better after she lost her virginity to a one-night stand. But when it comes down to it, saying things like that shows that women are bothered about it, I guess."

"You may be right." Sonoko was quiet for a while. It wasn't that she seemed to be thinking about something, but rather she appeared to be in a dilemma about voicing her opinion. "It often happens that the course of a woman's life is decided when she loses her virginity," she said, after a moment.

"I hadn't thought so deeply about it. So you mean . . ."

He closed his mouth, swallowing his words. He'd been about to say, "You're talking about yourself, right?" At the same time, thoughts of Mieko surfaced in his mind.

Sonoko changed the subject. "But are you so certain she's a virgin?"

"Well, there are times when I have my doubts and think the whole thing is just a charade."

"And you've been seeing her for over a year?"

"That's right. I'm just happy if she reacts in a convincing way."

Sonoko drained her glass and stood up. "Let's go. So, what do you think will happen in the end?"

Sasa hesitated again. "I don't know. There seems to be a young guy who flits in and out of her life, too."

"It all sounds pretty hectic," laughed Sonoko, and the two of them left the bar.

"Will you take me home? The roads are so dark, you see."

They began to walk. Partway along the narrow road was an unmanned railroad crossing. They could see four rails shining dully ahead of them. Taking care not to step on the rails in her sandals, Sonoko trod warily. As if it had suddenly occurred to her, she spoke out: "Still, I think the way you behave is really horrid."

Without saying anything, Sasa came to a halt, grabbed her arm and stopped her. Applying still more force, he guided her into an alleyway where he embraced her. With one hand, he tried to part the edges of her kimono. His fingers, now inside the garment, found their way with considerable difficulty to Sonoko's thighs. She struggled but made no attempt to shove him away; nor did she cry out.

"I'm going to give it to you good and hard."

He pushed his fingers in, if anything underscoring his roughness, and moved them about violently. The tips of his fingers gouged forcefully at the opening of her womb, which resembled a pair of thin lips. Sonoko groaned. Whether from pain or pleasure, now and then bursts of short words that made no sense mingled with the gasps.

The sound of a bell came to Sasa, and it was a while before he realized it was the railroad crossing. Before long, the rails began to vibrate and the noise seemed to last forever.

"I wonder if it's the last train. It should've passed by ages ago."

His wonderment was conveyed in his voice; his fingers stopped moving.

After a brief interval, Sonoko let out a sigh and said, in a slightly hoarse voice, "Freight trains run through the night."

Slowly disengaging herself from Sasa, she said, "Here is fine. I live close by."

Without waiting for his reply, she turned and strode briskly away. Her white, split-toed socks darted back and forth in the gloom, growing smaller and smaller as she receded into the distance.

ONE EVENING ABOUT A week later Sasa went to the bar where Sonoko worked. He could see her across the room, but she didn't get up and come over. After about twenty minutes, she sat down next to him without a word. The silence continued a while, then Sasa spoke. "Will you drink something?"

"Yes. I'll have a whisky soda."

She hurriedly finished the drink the bartender had made and set down in front of her, then got down from her stool at the counter.

"Are you leaving already?" enquired Sasa.

"Yes," she replied, brusquely. Stopping behind him, she drew her body close to him and whispered in his ear, "You're an awful person. You made me bleed."

Her tone was reproachful, but it was also tinged with ripe promise. Without looking back, Sonoko walked away.

Toward Dusk

Chapter 6   The Blackness Already There

THAT NIGHT SUGIKO WAS talkative. Seated across from
Sasa at a low dining table in the small tatami room, she sat relaxed, with her legs folded to the side, broaching one desultory
subject after another. The tea on the table was already cold.
The wall between the rooms had a small, round window with a
decorative bamboo lattice in it. Through the window she could
see the lower edge of the futon, already laid out.

As Sasa turned his head and looked at the window, all the
while conscious of Sugiko's gaze, she said, "I've had it with
places like this."

"Why?"

"You want to know why? I had an awful time on my way
home the other night, that's why. The taxi driver said a bunch
of nasty things to me."

That night, a week before, when Sasa tried to give Sugiko a
ride as usual, they had been blocked into the hotel's small car
park, and it seemed it would take quite a while to get out. In
the end, she had decided to take a taxi and catch the last train
home. It looked like they would be late for her last train by the
time they were free of the jam.

"You're talking about the last time we met? It was a good job
you made that train. You were just in time, right?"

"But the taxi driver . . ."

"What kind of things did he say?"

"He kept on saying things like 'Nice young ladies like you
oughtn't to go to hotels like that.' You know, that kind of thing."

— 185 —

"You shouldn't have picked up a taxi in front of the hotel, I guess. But, anyhow, you didn't have time to do anything else, did you?"

A young lady indeed, thought Sasa. This was tiresome, he muttered to himself. Sugiko's family were probably upper middle class. It was also true that without makeup she looked younger than she was.

The clothes and accessories she wore were modest, though on closer inspection, they seemed expensive.

"I'm tired of coming to places like this."

"Well, in that case, what should we do?"

"We don't need to do anything anymore."

Her tone of voice wasn't harsh but rather cynical.

"That's how you feel?"

Sasa, now on his feet, drew near her, seized one of her arms, and lifted her up, then forcefully opened the sliding door between this room and the next. Only a single futon had been laid out.

SUGIKO DIDN'T PUT ON the nightwear provided. She didn't even fold the clothes she'd taken off and instead piled them in one corner of the room and then got under the quilt. Pulling it up to their chins, they lay side by side on their backs. Sasa let his eyes wander lazily over the wood panelling of the ceiling.

Sugiko was, as ever, loquacious. Taking her left hand outside the quilt, she held it in front of her eyes.

"Well, don't you notice anything?"

Sasa's eyes were drawn to her nails, more so than to her five slender, attractive fingers, conscious that her nails had played a significant role in their relationship. Of the five, only the nail of her index finger had been clipped short and left jagged.

"Your nails, eh?" he said, gripping her right wrist and pulling her hand out from under the quilt. The nails on her right hand were all the same, uniform length. "Have you scratched someone again? The same thing happened before, didn't it?

Only that time the other nails had been pared short as well. But it's pretty roughly cut. Is that how he cut it?"

Sugiko's face turned towards him on the pillow.

"You don't miss a thing, do you?"

What she'd said caused something to stir within Sasa, but it soon passed.

"Why didn't you cut the other nails the same length, the way you did before? Did you leave them like that so you could scratch me?" He'd intended what he'd said to be a lighthearted joke.

"Don't you want to know?"

"Know what?"

"Who cut that nail?"

"Maybe."

"He's a young guy. A bit of fun to be with. He teases me all the time, and the way he talks is kind of smart." Sugiko began to explain of her own volition. "He's a bit of a tearaway and said he'd once tried to join a gang. He was even about to get a tattoo, but he decided not to go ahead."

"Maybe he just said that to show off."

Sugiko didn't say anything. Yet perhaps her relationship with an older man was the reason for her interest in young men of that type.

"This is twice now that somebody's pinned you down and cut your nails. Am I the only one who's been scratched without reacting violently?"

"But both times it was the same guy."

"The same guy? You mean the man I saw?"

"No."

The second time she'd left the nail of her index finger in the shape it had been cut by that man. Just as something began once again to stir within Sasa, Sugiko turned over and lay on her stomach, resting her chin on the backs of her linked hands. Then she broached a different topic.

"You know the other day? I stayed at my friend's house. She's a lesbian. I got scared about it."

"If she's a lesbian, there'd be no danger to that thing you do your best to protect all the time, would there?"

"She's the same age as me, and yet she's so experienced. It's really scary. She says leave it all to her, and she can even bring me to orgasm."

"Is it Yūko?"

"No."

Sugiko knew many young people Sasa had never met.

Without shifting position, she said, "I'm planning on living with her, so would you rent a room for us?"

"You've got to be kidding."

"I'm serious. You know, so the three of us can sleep together. First . . ." Sugiko had turned onto her side. Her face flushed, she wound her arms around Sasa and continued, "First, she and I would do it."

"What would I do?"

"You'd be alright just watching, wouldn't you? How about it, you'll rent a room?"

"I don't think so. But the three of us together does sound kind of interesting."

As he spoke, he held her naked shoulders between his palms and tried to flip her onto her back. Even now, he recalled the time he'd first gone to a hotel with Sugiko and how long it had taken before he'd overcome her determined resistance and drawn her naked body close to him, having stripped off all her clothes.

But what had left a far more lasting impression was the occasion when, exhausted from Sugiko's forceful attempts to push him aside, he'd decided to give it up and, half for fun, had brought his lips close to her lower body. As he did so, that part of her opened readily for him.

She had even wanted to adopt this posture in reverse. She used her lips and tongue deftly, and he guessed she'd had a fair amount of practice. Sasa realised that Sugiko, who evidently was experienced, was uninhibited when it came to sexual activity that stopped short of intercourse, so gradually he became more adventurous with her.

So long as they didn't engage in sexual intercourse itself, whatever extreme form of intimate behaviour a man and woman found themselves involved in, it would never amount to more than a fragile bond; no burdensome situation would arise from such a relationship. If anything, there would surely be an insufficient level of attachment. God had given conception and childbirth to women as their greatest role.

Conversely, it was also probably true that other than preventing the extinction of mankind, there was really no need for woman to exist at all, though of course that had been the case for hundreds of thousands of years. With the possibility of conception, that primeval blood would well up from deep within the woman when she mated with the male, and she regarded her relationship with the man as something imbued with special significance. With that thought in his mind, that link with conception caused Sasa's erection to fail.

Even when they lay atop one another, Sasa couldn't bring himself to watch Sugiko's expression of anguish, or perhaps pleasure. At times like that, he would secretly substitute Sugiko's face with that of another woman.

While watching a woman immersing herself in the depths of pleasure—a sensation incomparably deeper than that of a man—Sasa could almost feel a rocky desert of red soil stretching out around him. With his back to the entrance of their cliff cave home, with his body on top of a woman or perhaps behind one in the posture of an animal, he performed the sexual act, wide-eyed, all the while watching for signs of attack by beasts or reptiles. Eyes tightly shut, the woman leaves everything to the man. The nearby grass sways in the wind. The man tenses for an instant, the woman paying no heed. In that form, she had primeval blood within her.

When he lay on top of Sugiko, the seam of her closed thighs pressed in on him from both sides.

Something suddenly flashed across Sasa's mind. His dog had fallen ill, and he'd left it in the care of the vet.

I wonder when my dog will be home.

He adjusted his grip on the body that lay beneath him. *Would it transform into a wall of stone again today?* he wondered. She wouldn't allow an intrusion of that kind from any angle.

He was beginning to think there was something wrong with her. Sasa slowly lifted his hips from the seam of Sugiko's thighs and, just before their bodies separated, sank them deeply again. There was almost no resistance as he did so, and all too easily their bodies came together, joined in intercourse.

For a moment, Sasa was unable to grasp what had happened. It had been a week since he'd seen her. During that time had someone—perhaps the young man she'd mentioned earlier—made it possible?

Over the last eighteen months Sasa had often had his doubts. Had Sugiko been a virgin up to that point after all? He thought so. He mulled it over as if it had nothing to do with him. After a while, he pulled away.

"You weren't a virgin after all," he muttered, but he wasn't absolutely sure it had happened during the last week. It would have been an exaggeration to say the shock was so overpowering it had rendered him speechless, but he was nevertheless put into an abstracted frame of mind.

Sugiko was silent in the face of what he'd said. Her neck quivered for an instant, and her expression suggested she felt she'd been unfairly treated. The look soon disappeared, and, drawing her body close again and clinging to him, she whispered in Sasa's ear, "You can treat me roughly."

THEY LEFT THE HOTEL in Sasa's car. Sugiko's talkativeness had deserted her, and she simply sat quietly in the seat next to him. Sasa sensed a dark, vague presence between them, but he didn't consider giving the presence form by enquiring about it. It was already a thing of the past, and he was relieved that his responsibility had halved by dint of sharing Sugiko with that dark presence.

"I'm a wicked woman," she said. Whether it was because she could no longer bear the silence or whether she wanted Sasa to ask her about that man, he wasn't sure.

"Why?"

"Because I've been seeing two men at the same time."

"It doesn't matter. I don't mind you doing that sort of thing."

He sounded halfhearted. What he'd intended to say in a consoling tone turned into a voice seeking to affirm his own sense of security.

It had gone ten in the evening. Dozens of lights twinkled on the wide, asphalt road, and the headlights of Sasa's car moved through them. In the past, quarrels had often erupted at times like this. They usually involved Sasa saying he was tired and was only prepared to see her as far as the terminal station and how he would like her to go along with that. And Sugiko would tell him in no uncertain terms she wanted him to drive her home. On occasions such as those, she was terribly stubborn, and in the end Sasa would give in.

But tonight he drove straight along the route to his house, stopping only at a station along the way. Reaching over, he opened the door on Sugiko's side, and said, "I'll take you this far tonight."

She got out of the car without demur. After closing the door from inside, Sasa put his foot on the accelerator and slowly drove forward. But the traffic lights ten metres or so ahead turned red, so he brought the car to a halt there. While waiting for the green light, he turned and looked in Sugiko's direction and saw her from the back. It was the sort of late March weather that looked as if it might rain, though the inside of the station was bright. As she walked through that light toward the ticket barrier, Sugiko had one hand shoved in the pocket of her cream-colored raincoat. The hem flared out, and the colour appeared strangely sombre.

With exaggerated movements, she turned her head to the left and then to the right, and her hair, which had been cut short above the nape of her neck, waved. Her appearance and the way she carried herself suggested a slovenly demeanour.

In his mind's eye, a dark film had enveloped Sugiko. Within the layer of dirty, grey air perfectly fused to the outline of her body a centimetre deep, were an unfamiliar young man and Sasa himself.

Chapter 7   Toward Dusk

IN THE AFTERNOON, ON the day he'd arranged to meet Sugiko, there was a telephone call from Yūko.

"Something's happened, and I must see you. I'm quite worried."

"That sounds a bit serious. Can't you tell me on the phone?"

"Are you alone?"

Sasa was alone in his room.

"Yes, I am."

"Anyhow, won't you meet me?" said Yūko.

"I want you to tell me at least the gist of it now."

"Well, alright. Sugiko turned on the gas in her room. They called an ambulance, and, well, it was just awful."

An image of Sugiko when he'd left her at the station a week before came to mind: her slovenly gait and the hem of her twisted, billowing raincoat. But he couldn't bring himself to take what Yūko had said at face value.

"Oh, I see," he replied vaguely.

"Aren't you shocked?"

"Yes. So, did she die?"

"Did she die? What a way to put it!"

"I'm concerned."

"No, she didn't die. Anyhow, come meet me, will you?"

Yūko mentioned a foreign-sounding name.

"What are you talking about?"

"It's a well-known boutique. They have a tearoom in the store, so why don't we meet there?"

"It might be well-known to you and your friends, but I can't go into a store like that alone."

"Sasa-san, you've bought your daughter toys before, haven't you?"

"What is this all of a sudden?"

"Even as an adult, you were fond of toys, isn't that right? Don't you remember? One time you gave Sugiko and me a frog."

"A frog?"

"Yes. A small frog with a spring mechanism. You put it on the table and after a minute or so it jumps really high in the air."

Yūko gave another foreign-sounding name. "I wonder if you know the big toy store."

"If that's the place you mean, then I know it."

"Wait inside there. The boutique is right nearby."

"It seems we do need to meet after all."

"I think so."

She hung up.

AS HE APPROACHED THE toy store, Sasa heard a woman's voice calling his name. He stopped and turned around, just as Yūko almost collided with him. There was a feminine scent about her.

"I called you over and over, and then you stopped suddenly like that."

Having spotted Sasa, Yūko had broken into a trot as she drew near him. Her body was ever so slightly moist with sweat.

"The boutique is just over there, see?"

"So it is."

Still standing where he'd stopped, Sasa's nostrils distended in response to Yūko's scent. There was little body odour about her. Then again, every woman exudes a slight odour that rises from her skin, under which are her internal organs and her womb and ovaries. The smells of body and perfume compete

— 194 —

with one another, and when the perfume is internalised it becomes the woman's scent. Sugiko gave off such a smell, too, though it had yet to reach maturity. Yūko, on the other hand, must have had all kinds of experiences.

"What's the matter? Let's go," she urged.

They set off together. Yūko paused in front of a small building about fifty metres ahead. In the first-floor display window was a mannequin whose skin had been painted black. A white cloth was wrapped around its head, and it wore a floral-pattern long dress.

"Here we are."

She pushed open the door. Apart from the mezzanine, which was used as a tearoom, the store was open to the ceiling. Sitting across from Yūko, Sasa could look out over the handrail at the store's interior. It was quiet. Gazing below, he could see four or five steps leading to the basement sales floor. There was no sign of customers or shop assistants amid the myriad of colours.

"The place is deserted."

"Mm. It's an expensive store, that's why."

"Can they get by like this, I wonder."

Without answering his question, Yūko lowered her voice, "So, about Sugiko . . . ," she said, falling silent again for a while.

Sasa waited for her to continue. Without touching on the circumstances around Sugiko's attempted suicide, she said, "I think right now Sugiko needs to get away from everything for a while."

"You may be right."

Sasa stared at Yūko, but their eyes didn't meet. With her gaze lowered to the cup on the table, she continued as if she were talking to herself. "I'm thinking of taking her on a boat trip or something like that."

"A boat trip? Where to?"

She mentioned an island, a well-known tourist destination they could reach after a five- or six-hour cruise.

As before, their eyes didn't meet. Her tone suggested she was talking discreetly about some serious problem, but she sounded half-hearted.

"I would appreciate it if you would," ventured Sasa.

Assuming the incident involving Sugiko had actually occurred, he wondered if he'd be left with a considerable burden and what the young man's attitude would be. But he said something else. "Why do you suppose she did a thing like that?"

"I think she was tired. It was just on impulse."

Sasa felt partly responsible for that too. "When did it happen?"

"Two days ago."

Sugiko's family wouldn't have wanted anything to do with Yūko. Her parents would hardly have been happy to find she was their daughter's friend.

Given the state she was in, would they allow her to go on a trip with a friend like that? They might not even know of Yūko's existence.

And yet Sasa said, "Please take her on holiday, won't you?" His voice sounded noncommittal again. "If it's a tourist destination, won't the island be a little too crowded? There's another island beyond that one, isn't there? That might be better."

"Maybe. Yes, I think you might be right."

Taking out several banknotes, he handed them discreetly to Yūko, saying, "I hope this will help you make the trip."

The money was only enough to cover their travel and a night in a hotel. Yūko took it without saying anything and, hesitating for a moment, put it in her handbag.

"I think she'll be better in a month."

"A month?"

"I'll have her call you then."

Sasa looked around the tearoom as he listened to Yūko. There were dozens of customers in all sorts of combinations— a man and a woman, two women, two women and a man—but he didn't see any men together.

"Let's leave," he urged, standing up. As they moved away from the table, Yūko staggered slightly, as if her leg had gone numb. Sasa grasped her upper arm and supported her, her resilient flesh pushing back against his hands.

EMERGING ONTO THE SIDEWALK, Sasa had mixed feelings. He stopped for a moment and looked at Yūko. Yūko returned his gaze and ventured, "Do you fancy a quick look in the toy store? Come on, let's go."

They moved off. Sasa's pace was sluggish; something was on his mind, making him tread even more lethargically.

"Slow down, will you?" he asked.

The store's richly coloured, vertical sign gradually grew bigger. In his childhood Sasa was hardly ever given toys. It wasn't that his family was short of money; it was more likely his parents didn't believe in spoiling him with toys. In those days he would occupy himself by making tanks out of old wooden cotton reels and firing rubber bullets from guns made of disposable chopsticks. As he played like this, he decided that one day he would buy a toy store. While he had completely lost that desire, he still became excited whenever he went into one.

"Sasa-san."

At the sound of Yūko's voice, he stopped just as he was about to pass the toy store. He paused for a moment at the automatic doors, and when he stepped inside, a peal of laughter resounded throughout the shop. It sounded like the slightly hoarse voice of an old man, and its amplitude, modulation, and lack of reserve were extraordinary. It sounded as if someone in the store had suddenly lost his mind. Sasa stood bolt upright and looked about.

Yūko prodded his shoulder with a finger.

"It's that old man over there, see."

"Old man? You mean he's gone off his rocker?"

"That's awful! It's a toy, silly."

She pointed to the wall on the left, towards the back of the room. An old man's head was hanging there, like the head of some wild beast or antelope put on display in a hunter's drawing room. A crowd of people had gathered and were looking at it.

"How come you had it figured right away?"

"Because its voice isn't human."

The laughter continued.

"But it doesn't sound like a mechanical voice either."

"It's a recorded voice, that's why. There's a resonance from magnetic tape mixed in."

"Hmm," he agreed.

Drawing near and taking a closer look, he found that it had the brown face of an Asian man with dozens of wrinkles carved into its surface and was about half the size of a human face. Faded brown hair stuck out from both sides of a flat, green cap. The ends of the red cloth wound about its neck were tied in a bow.

A middle-aged foreign man reached out a long arm and tugged on the red cloth where it was knotted. From between its thin, dark brown lips, parted widely, the tip of a flat, muddy-coloured tongue moved just a short way slowly in and out, and the laughter began again. The tiny mechanism within was replaying the recording. Only the upper lids of the small eyes repeatedly drooped and opened again, looking like bird's eyes.

The doleful voice continued in a variety of intonations for a while. Though it was certainly laughter, it changed over and over from a tone of derision to self-contempt and again to a voice full of malediction. Just as Sasa began to worry that the mechanism had gone wrong and the tape would never end, the laughter, which had begun to increase in pitch even further, stopped abruptly, as if it had been shut down. It seemed Sasa's solicitude had been treated with contempt.

In that instant the thing that had been lurking in a corner of his mind since the phone call from Yūko suddenly grew larger. He took a slow, deep breath.

A bittersweet smell lingered in the air, but he couldn't tell whether it came from the innumerable new toys or whether it had drifted from the back of his own nose. An image of himself as a child came to mind, walking towards the red sky. At the end of the road was a black house silhouetted against the sunset. He felt as though his stomach was burning and shrivelling up by the heat of a charcoal fire. In the meantime, the bittersweet smell rose up from the back of his nose.

Suddenly he was aware of the high-pitched voice of a young man as he approached the face. "You seem to be having a rough day today!" He laughed, tugging on the red cloth again. Two or three friends with him laughed along lightheartedly, but the recorded laughter droned on tediously and drowned them out. Then, again, the voice stopped abruptly.

With a forced laugh, Sasa pointed at the wall and said to a middle-aged sales clerk standing nearby, "I'll take one of those, please."

His expression remaining serious, the sales clerk said, "We have an old woman, too."

"An old woman, you say?"

"I'm talking about the toy."

"No, the old man is just fine."

Sasa carried the bag with the head in one hand.

The automatic doors slid open in front of him, and when he went outside the sky was aglow with the setting sun. It was the kind of bright red sky that came just before a dull, colourless dusk. Standing still, he gazed at the sky, and Yūko soon drew close to him.

"What's the matter?"

"Nothing."

"Shall we walk to the main street?"

Without replying, he indicated the paper bag in his hand, and said, "This old guy's popular, don't you think? The minute he stops laughing someone comes along and yanks his necktie. At that rate he'd be laughing all day long."

"I guess so. You're rather frivolous, buying it like that."

"I wouldn't say I'm frivolous really."

Under one of the trees lining the street a short distance from the store he turned to Yūko and said, "I was thinking about something strange. You can't really call this a toy, either. I wonder where it was made?"

Yūko replied, "It's made in Korea, of course."

"How do you know?"

"Because when I went there the other day I thought it was fun and asked the sales clerk about it."

"Was it laughing all the time in that weird voice then as well?"

"Uh-huh."

"It was you that told me to wait in that store, right?"

"Uh-huh."

"Was that your idea? Or did Sugiko have something to do with it?"

With a suspicious look on her face, Yūko leaned back lightly against the tree trunk.

"Sasa-san, what are you trying to say?" She spoke in an unhurried manner. He looked at her again. She was a tall woman and fairly heavily made-up. She wore black boots. Her face altered slightly, and she looked at him out of the corner of her eye. Her gaze was fixed on him.

"What are you trying to say?"

"Sasa-san, are you going somewhere now?"

"Not really."

"Why not come back to my place for a bit?"

Yūko's scent seemed to have grown stronger. Her piercing eyes were becoming pale and dry, and for an instant they gave off an intense gleam.

Suddenly feeling tired, Sasa said, "Let's forget about it. So, Sugiko was fine after all, was she?"

Yūko didn't reply.

"That's good then."

Holding the paper bag in front of her, he said, "I'll give this to you. You can give it to Sugiko," he added, turning and walking away.

When Sasa went into the dining room that day, having woken up as he always did in the afternoon, his wife was drinking tea with Naoko. It was a Sunday.

"Have you finished lunch?"

"We're about to have it now. It's been a while since you ate with Naoko."

"I suppose so. What are you having?"

"I was just saying I wonder whether I should make French toast."

"I'll have that too. Make it savoury," he said.

His wife countered with a cutting remark. "Is there such a thing as savoury French toast? Are you of a mind to let Naoko eat something like that?"

"I'm not saying Naoko has to eat it too. Besides, making it savoury doesn't necessarily make it salty."

"But there's no such thing as savoury French toast."

"It doesn't matter what you call it, does it? All I'm asking is that you make it savoury."

"I'd have thought someone who does what you do would care what something is called."

"There are times when it matters and times when it doesn't."

"Oh, really?"

His wife stood up and went into the kitchen. Naoko quietly looked the other way. Having begun to get worked up about it, Sasa regained his composure. That kind of thing happened from time to time. He knew his wife was criticising him in a roundabout way.

A week had gone by since he'd met with Yūko, but he'd heard nothing. That was to be expected, and, while he'd tried to put Sugiko out of his thoughts, when all was said and done she was ever present in a corner of his mind.

He wondered when the young man, whose name and face he didn't know, had made an appearance in Sugiko's life. Though he wasn't certain, he was fairly sure the man was single. Because Sugiko was attempting to fill a void in the young man's life, she had no time to meet with Sasa, and in fact seeing him was a drawback for her. Perhaps Sugiko's desire to escape her involvement with two men at the same time was at the heart of it.

In the final analysis, he guessed that was what Yūko had wanted to tell him.

Before long, a plate was set down in front of him. The yellowish bread on the plate looked untoasted. Sasa preferred it a little browned, but he didn't say anything.

He returned to his room and tried reading a book for a while, but he wasn't taking any of it in. Since he'd reached a decision about Sugiko, there was no point calling Yūko.

From the outset, he hadn't tried to discover Sugiko's telephone number.

Mieko's face sprang to mind unbeckoned. She hadn't phoned for about a month, as she usually did. He had written down her number, and taking out his notebook, he stared at it for a while. He didn't know if she'd be home. Although Mieko had said she lived alone, Sasa had never called her.

For pretty much the last two years, she'd called about once a month and they would meet in a hotel. She was always in a topsy-turvy state; Sasa felt he was being used as a sedative. Gazing at the number in his notebook, he wondered whether he, a middle-aged man, wanted more out of his relationship with her. Mieko was the same age as Sugiko.

His own life was in turmoil, and this unsatisfactory state of affairs was certainly irksome. It was just like having a drink.

That was how he felt about seeing Mieko, and perhaps she felt the same way, too.

He began to dial her number. He heard the sound of the phone ringing and then the receiver being lifted. When he heard Mieko's voice, he realized he'd missed her terribly.

"Can't you meet me today?"

"I was going to call you yesterday, but I'm busy this evening."

"Busy?"

"Yes. I'm meeting someone."

"What time?"

"Five."

"You could cancel."

"It's an appointment I can't change."

"You're seeing that guy you call your fiancé?"

"It's someone else. It's not just the two of us, you see."

"It's just after two. If you're seeing him at five, you've time to see me first, haven't you?"

"Even if I set off right away, we'd only have a little over an hour."

"That's long enough, isn't it?" Sasa sensed hesitation. "Is your mother there?"

"She's already gone out. She's going there directly."

Sasa was pretty sure it was an *o-miai*, the first step toward a possible arranged marriage. It seemed Mieko wasn't lying when she said she'd tried calling him.

"Come on, let's get together."

"But today . . ."

"I'm not bothered by anything like that."

Normally one to give up right away if he was turned down, Sasa persisted in his efforts to entice her out. Underlying Mieko's words too was a hint of something that suggested she couldn't altogether refuse him.

Seemingly perplexed, she suddenly said in a clear voice, "Alright then."

"I'll see you at the usual hotel, then."

Sasa removed his wristwatch and placed it on the bed-table in the hotel room. Women disliked it when men spent the time with them looking at their watches, though on this occasion there was no need to stand on ceremony. As always, Mieko cried out in a raw voice from the bed. Her smile-like expression at the moment she received him was no doubt genuine, but the expression that followed—coming as it did from the movement of the eyebrows, the lips and nostrils—looked as though it could be stripped off like a mask.

The hollow, blue-tinged cheeks of a woman long ago flashed across his mind and then disappeared. Sometimes Mieko's closed eyes looked as though they were slightly open. She had been trained to produce that crude voice by her first lover, the one she called her fiancé, whom she said she'd met about a year before Sasa. Sasa wondered whether her subdued voice would spontaneously change one day into a high-pitched, lingering cry.

Sasa could see a light grey film under Mieko's skin. Her skin couldn't be called delicate, but if you ran your fingertips slowly across it they would slip smoothly along. Perhaps she had poor muscle tone, and the indendations from the pressure of his fingers against her skin vanished only slowly.

Mieko behaved enthusiastically, and it wasn't merely for Sasa's benefit either. She seemed obsessed with making something out of their relationship, and her eagerness was readily apparent. There are women that perspire lightly as they lie motionless, each drop of their sweat densely concentrated, but Mieko wasn't like that.

"I'm tired."

She lay face down, a large pillow wedged beneath her chest.

Looking at his watch, Sasa said, "We've only another ten minutes."

"That's OK."

Mieko lay in the same position without moving.

"Why don't you take a shower?"

"I'm OK like this. I'll take all the smells of this room with me. You'd like that, wouldn't you, Sasa-san?"

After getting dressed, Sasa sat in the chair and gazed at her. At last, getting off the bed, she began to put her clothes on with unhurried movements.

"You know Sugiko, don't you?" began Sasa.

"Uh-huh. But she's not really one of my friends. I don't even think she has many friends, now you mention it."

"Have you heard anything of her?"

"You'd know better than anyone, wouldn't you?"

He didn't say anything.

"Come to think of it, I did hear recently she was chasing around after a young guy."

"When was that?"

"Mm, when was it?"

Reaching both hands behind her, she tried to hook her fingertips around the tab of the zipper. Standing and drawing near, Sasa zipped the fastener up in one stroke.

"About five days ago."

"Five days ago?"

Bending over to put her shoes on, Mieko said, "Ah, I see. That explains why you phoned me for the first time."

Sasa didn't reply.

Opening the door, they went out into the corridor. Mieko would probably be a little late.

ONE EVENING, ABOUT TEN days later, there was a telephone call from Yūko.

"Are you alone?" she said as always.

"Yes. How was the trip?" enquired Sasa.

After hesitating a moment, she replied, "We went to the island you recommended. Sugiko was able to settle down and relax, too. She says she wants to see you."

"See me?"

"Mm."

"If she wants to see me, then there's nothing for it, I suppose."

There was another brief silence.

"She says she wants to meet you, so she asked me to call and let you know."

Until then he'd nearly always met Sugiko on a Saturday. They would arrange to meet in the lobby of a city-centre hotel and then go on to a love hotel.

"Well, she said to tell you to meet at the usual place this Saturday."

She hung up.

When he saw her that day at the place they'd arranged to meet, Sugiko's face was a little taut around her cheeks, and while her lips moved no sound came from her mouth.

Sasa wore the same facial expression he always did. Aware of his gaze, Sugiko adopted a similar expression, and her demeanour became even more affected than that of Sasa.

"What do you fancy eating?"

He'd been thinking they'd just have a meal together and then go their separate ways.

"Chicken," replied Sugiko.

They went down the steps leading to the basement car park.

There was a small poultry restaurant a short distance away from the city centre. The owner was a difficult person, but Sasa had been a regular customer for a long while. The middle-aged man, who was also a bit of a playboy, seemed pleased Sasa had brought Sugiko along with him and, if anything, he was in a cheerful mood.

Pulling open the glass door, they heard the owner shooing something away. Sasa assumed he was being turned away and looked at the owner.

The owner smiled when he saw Sugiko and turned to Sasa and said, "Why! It's been a long time."

"That gave me a fright. I thought we were going to be turned away. Was it a cat?"

"No. A bush warbler."

A cage, housing the bird, was hanging from the ceiling in one corner of the restaurant.

"What did it do?"

"It got up to some mischief."

What kind of mischief would a bush warbler get into? wondered Sasa.

"The tatami room is free," said the owner.

Though he referred to it as a room, it was actually a small, tatami-floored area, visible from the counter. As they sat on either side of the small table, the food was brought out. Sugiko always had a hearty appetite, and that evening was no exception.

Resting his chopsticks, Sasa gazed at her, marvelling at her vitality.

Sasa felt almost as if the very existence of this woman had permeated every inch of his body, like a fine film of oil, over the year and a half or so he'd been seeing her. The layers thus formed barely adhered to him. Yet if he were to stop seeing her they would peel away as time went by, and before very long they would be no more than a faded recollection with no sense of reality at all. That much was plain. In the meantime, he supposed there would be a short time when, suddenly, the feel of Sugiko's skin, her odour and her various attitudes would press in on him, but after a year or so, if he got past that, they would fade to distant memories.

Sasa watched her.

Before long, the meal came to an end, and with it the evening. He knew the time had come to end his relationship with Sugiko too.

He started to speak.

"Is there something you want to say?" Putting her head to one side slightly, a smile played on Sugiko's lips, and she said, quietly, "Sleep with me."

Having drawn back momentarily, those words began to excite him.

As they were leaving the restaurant, the owner called out, "Next time let's go to a bar and have a drink together. What do you say?"

"What about the restaurant?" laughed Sasa.

"We'll have to close early I guess," said the owner, laughing too.

It had grown dark outside; a hint of spring was in the air.

As they got into the car, Sugiko said, "Where are we going?"

Sasa ought to have replied that he would take her to a nearby station and leave her off there. But, what he actually said was, "What shall we do?"

"I don't really mind."

Sugiko's words opened the door to a more troublesome situation than ever before. Sasa was indecisive.

"Let's go for a drive."

With no clear idea of where they were headed, he drove the car toward a quiet, dimly lit area, and then realised that subconsciously he was looking for a place to lose himself in a while. Thick concrete posts stood in rows along both sides of the road, like an avenue lined with trees. It was the road beneath the same expressway he'd driven on once before with Sugiko. He recalled there was a harbour in the neighbourhood where cargo ships docked.

If they came out at the quay, the night would be illuminated by dozens of lights, and the surface of the sea would, he supposed, be covered with the glittering white crests of the waves. He imagined he would be able to rid his mind of this dangerous ambiguity once confronted by such scenery. They turned left off the road beneath the expressway, right onto the road dead ahead and then left again. Street lamps lined the wide road, and the number of pedestrians dwindled until, eventually, both cars and people had disappeared.

They turned left and left again, and just when he thought the port would come into view a vast expanse of black water suddenly appeared before them. Resembling a blackboard, the surface shone dimly, as if it had been coated in oil.

"Where are we?" said Sugiko.

The car seemed to have entered another world before they realised it. The blacktop extended right up to the waterfront. Driving slowly across its surface, he stopped just where the asphalt ran out. There wasn't another car around.

"I wonder what that red light is."

Sugiko extended a finger towards the windscreen. A single red light shone through the gloom, about a hundred metres off to the right. A small building facing a man-made harbour wall, which enclosed the water in a large curve, came into view.

"It's an electric light, isn't it?"

"What do you think it is?"

"A police box, I would guess. Looks like it was built facing the water."

The landscape in front of them began to return to something with an aspect of reality. As Sasa had suspected, this was probably part of the harbour. It was set back from the sea, and the surface of the water inside the breakwater was calm; perhaps it was used to land freight from the cargo ships. Immediately beyond the car's hood they could see a large, mushroom-shaped object that looked as though it was growing out of the asphalt; it was probably an iron bollard used to secure mooring lines.

"I thought we'd come out by the brightly lit jetty, but . . ."

"Well, it's not dark here, though it is a weird sort of grey light."

The outlines of people and objects were clearly illuminated. The air was filled with a pale grey luminescence which seemed to pervade the space around them. Sasa had seen light like this somewhere before. His sexual desire slowly began to build and grow in intensity. Stubbing out the cigarette he'd been smoking in the ashtray, he reached out the same hand toward Sugiko and pressed his palm against her breast.

"What is that?" She looked at the back of his hand.

As soon as he put his arm around her shoulder and tried to draw her towards him, he heard the hard click of a lock opening. Sugiko opened the door, leaping out of the car as if she'd been sprung from a trap. She ran toward the black water.

Surely she's not going to jump in, he thought.

She began running in a wide curve in the opposite direction. Had Sasa's half-hearted advances caused something within Sugiko to snap?

It seemed, after all, that Sasa's attitude was no different from that of the young man. Had her recent recollection of the young man been superimposed on him? Though seized with self-loathing as he recalled his own behaviour, he was incensed at the way she had reacted. She ran sluggishly; she moved her arms and legs vigorously, yet her rate of advance was painfully slow. To him she resembled a water-filled bag slopping about on the asphalt, an image spawned perhaps by his rage turning to hatred.

"Run all you like, why don't you?" he yelled as he started the car.

He drove at a right angle to Sugiko, and the distance between them abruptly increased. He realised then that the station was quite a distance and there would be no taxis in such a dark, deserted place as this.

He did a U-turn. Returning to the original spot, he came upon an unexpected sight. Sugiko was still running as though the soles of her shoes were sticking to the ground, and a bicycle was following her. Holding a red torch aloft in one hand, a uniformed policeman gained on her, his white bicycle rocking wildly from side to side as he pumped the pedals. Sasa found himself pursuing the bicycle in his car. Turning around and noticing him, the policeman put a whistle to his mouth and blew strongly into it.

This is a damned nuisance, Sasa thought. With an even greater sense of aversion, he was seized by an impulse to drive off. What followed was probably more to do with his reflexive action than the prudence of a middle-aged man. As he over-took the bicycle, the noise from the police whistle became louder still, producing a sound not unlike that of a tin whistle.

After driving about five metres past Sugiko, who was still running, Sasa stopped the car and threw open the passenger-side door. Heaving himself out of his seat, he leaned towards the opening and called out in a calm voice, "Get in."

Sugiko stopped running and climbed in. Just as she did so, the policeman got off his white bicycle and stood it up by the car.

"Oh, I see," he said, absentmindedly, and then, peering into the interior of the car, enquired of Sugiko, "A friend of yours?"

Sugiko nodded emphatically.

"We've had a slight row," said Sasa, turning toward the policeman. He was a young man, about twenty, with a broad face.

"You don't say. Anyhow, let me see your driver's licence."

Shining the red light of his torch on the driver's licence that Sasa had handed to him, the policeman copied down the particulars in his notebook.

Handing the licence to Sugiko, he shone the torch inside the car, and said, "You're a nice young couple, so you ought to behave civilly with each other."

"Yes, officer."

Sasa heard Sugiko's reply.

Sasa wished he could hide in the darkness of the corner by the driver's seat. The red light wasn't bright enough for the policeman to easily discern the details, and he seemed to have overlooked the date of birth on the driver's licence. Sasa supposed he was trying to act like an adult. His face was covered with pimples, and he guessed that a twenty-year-old might not find it strange for Sugiko to be with a man four or five years her senior. Decades ago, Sasa had had the same experience.

Starting the car, this time Sasa searched out the bright lights of the city. He remained quiet, and Sugiko too stared ahead, her body tense.

The station platform slid into view. It looked like a bridge adorned with lights and was unexpectedly high up.

"I wonder which station that is. You're going to have to climb a lot of steps," muttered Sasa.

"Are you dropping me off there?" she said.

"I think it best."

"I won't get out."

"Oh yes you will."

The station building came in sight, suddenly looming large.

"You eat two meals a day, right, Sasa-san?"

"Huh?"

"How many times a day does your wife eat?"

"Three I guess. But what are you getting at?"

"What time does your wife eat lunch?"

"About two, I should think. But what are you . . . ?"

They approached the railroad bridge, and Sasa stopped the car in front of it. Across the road, off to the right, they could see the brightly lit ticket office.

"I won't get out, I tell you," she repeated. "If you drop me here, I'll phone your wife. Around noon."

"You'll phone? And say what?"

"I'll say, 'Mr. Sasa's residence? Please let him know. . . .'"

"Let him know what?"

"Emori Sugiko is dead."

After a brief silence, Sasa said, "We mustn't quarrel. Isn't that what the policeman said?"

"If I get out here, then we won't be able to quarrel anymore."

After lapsing into silence again for a while, Sasa said, "You're a nice young couple. That's what the policeman said, right? Ha! Well, the young couple has broken up already, I heard."

"What are you talking about?"

"The young guy you had a fight with, that's what."

"I don't know anyone like that."

Her words may have been spoken calmly, but Sasa felt the woman in them.

"As I said, you'd better get out here. Before long, you'll be able to go back to your old life. Then you can start a family."

He wasn't simply trying to appease her. When all was said and done, he knew that sort of life would suit a woman like Sugiko. If anything, the appearance and disappearance of the young man had provided her with an antidote to the kind of life he was leading with her. Reaching out, he hooked his fingertips around the door lock on her side. He waited for her reaction. Her body swayed slightly, that was all. Otherwise she was quiet. He leaned into her, and his face brushed her hair.

He was allured by the proximity of her slightly sweaty skin. For a moment he hesitated. There was a low metallic sound as the door lock opened.

First Japanese Publication Information

"Burning Dolls" (人形を焼く) first published in *Bijutsu Techō*, no. 139, April, 1958.

"The Molester" (痴) first published in *Chi·Kōsuibin*, Gakushū Kenkyūsha, May, 1964.

"At the Aquarium" (水族館にて) first published in *Fujin Asahi*, vol. 11, no. 2, February, 1956.

"Treatment" (治療) first published in *Gunzō*, vol. 9, no. 1, January, 1954.

"Straw Wedding Ceremony" (藁婚式) first published in *Bungakukaigi*, no. 6, December, 1948.

"Midnight Stroll" (深夜の散歩) first published in *Ōru Yomimono*, vol. 14, no. 10, October, 1959.

"Flowers" (花束) first published in *Gunzō*, vol. 18, no. 5, May, 1963.

"Voice of Spring" (春の声) first published in *Bungakukai*, Vol. 20, No. 3, March, 1966.

"A Bad Summer" (悪い夏) first published in *Shinchō*, vol. 53, no. 8, August, 1956.

"Toward Dusk" (夕暮まで) first published in complete form by Shinchōsha, September, 1978.

About the Contributors

Andrew Clare, a partner in a commercial law firm, lives with his family near Manchester, England. A graduate of Sheffield University (B.A., Japanese Studies) and Kobe University (Master of Political Science), his literary tastes include the novels of sensual writer Nagai Kafū, the proletarian author Kobayashi Takiji, and Endō Shūsaku, amongst other modern Japanese writers. He has translated Matsumoto Seichō's 1961 legal thriller, *Pro Bono* (Vertical, Inc.), and a variety of short stories.

James Dorsey teaches Japanese literature, culture, and language at Dartmouth College. His first book was *Critical Aesthetics: Kobayashi Hideo, Modernity, and Wartime Japan* (Harvard University Asia Center, 2009). He also co-edited (with Doug Slaymaker) the book *Literary Mischief: Sakaguchi Ango, Culture, and the War* (Lexington Books, 2010). It includes two essays and four translations by him.

He is currently pursuing two research projects. The first focuses on how the December 1941 attack on Pearl Harbor was depicted in wartime Japan; the second is a study of the political folk song movement in Japan during the late 1960s.

In his free time he likes to ride his bicycle through either the backstreets of Tokyo or the muddy hills of New Hampshire. He is also an avid (though not particularly good) practitioner of aikido.

About the Artist

Kyōsuke Tchinai (智内兄助) was born in 1948 in Ehime, Japan. In 1966, he graduated from Imabari-Nishi high school, and entered the National University of Fine Arts. He received several distinguished awards including The Prize for Excellence at the young Japanese Painters' Exhibition, 1988, and The Yasui Award, 1991. From 1981 onwards, he participated in large group exhibitions such as The Cleveland Biennial (USA), the Ueno-no-Mori Grand Prix Exhibition (Japan), and the Yasui Award Exhibition (Japan).

Since 1983, he has held major solo exhibitions at the Tokyo Central Art Museum, the Kitakata Museum, Japan, the Kuma Museum, the Nakata Museum, Takashimaya and the Ehime Fine Arts Museum. In 2000, he signed an exclusive worldwide contract with the Tamenaga Gallery, which has already organized two solo exhibitions in their Paris gallery. The works of Tchinai are kept in many Japanese museums (Aichi, Imabari, Saitama, Kariya, etc.) as well as in private collections, including that of Baroness Ariane de Rothschild.

CPSIA information can be obtained at www.ICGtesting.com
Printed in the USA
BVOW030816111212

307876BV00002B/40/P